現代聊齋故事

天 堂 遊

A Visit to Heaven

漢 英 對 照

馬 德 五 著譯

Tom Te-Wu Ma

文史哲出版社印行

國家圖書館出版品預行編目資料

天堂遊：**A Visit to Heaven** / 馬德五著譯. --
初版 -- 臺北市：文史哲,民 99.11
頁；　公分. --（文學叢刊；239）

ISBN 978-957-549-933-4 (平裝)

857.6　　　　　　　　　　99021444

文 學 叢 刊 239

天堂遊 A Visit to Heaven

著 譯 者：馬　　　德　　　五
出 版 者：文 史 哲 出 版 社
　　　　　http://www.lapen.com.tw
　　　　　e-mail：lapen@ms74.hinet.net
登記證字號：行政院新聞局版臺業字五三三七號
發 行 人：彭　　　正　　　雄
發 行 所：文 史 哲 出 版 社
印 刷 者：文 史 哲 出 版 社
　　　　　臺北市羅斯福路一段七十二巷四號
　　　　　郵政劃撥帳號：一六一八○一七五
　　　　　電話886-2-23511028・傳真886-2-23965656

實價新臺幣二八○元

中華民國九十九年（2010）十一月初版

天　堂　遊

目　次

2　天堂遊

天　堂　遊
（A Visit to Heaven）

第一章　Chapter One

"到了，"織成放鬆了泰林的手，愉快地告訴他，"你可以睜開眼睛啦。我們已經在天堂的門口了。"

"Here we are," Ze-chen said as she released Tai-lin's hand and happily told him, "now, you may open your eyes. We are at the gate of Heaven."

泰林睜開眼一看，驚喜地發現他們站在一座鉅大的金色牌樓門口，牌樓的最上端有三個紅色大字："南天門"。

After opening his eyes, Tai-lin was overjoyed to find that they were standing in front of a huge golden gate with three big red words at the very top: "Southern Heaven Gate".

他曾經在書上讀到過，有四個進口去到天堂，南天門是距離中國最近的一個。可泰林做夢也不會想到居然有一天他也能來到這個名叫天堂的神秘地方。

He had read some books that claimed there were four

entrances to Heaven, and Southern Heaven Gate was the closest one to China. But Tai-lin never dreamed that he would one day come to the mysterious place called Heaven.

當泰林正在懷疑是否是在夢中時,他驚駭地發現兩隻幾乎和人一樣高的全白色老虎緩慢地可也很不友善地向他走來,老虎的牙齒外露並發出低沉的吼聲。泰林立刻後退,織成及時走來擋住了老虎的前進,她用手輕拍一隻老虎的頭頂,告訴這兩隻動物泰林是她的客人,她會負責他的天堂之行的。老虎似信非信地望了泰林一下,然後很不情願地走回到南天門的兩側安靜地坐了下來,謹慎地望著泰林跟著織成走進了天堂。

While he wondered if he was dreaming, Tai-lin was startled by two all-white tigers almost as tall as a man walking toward him slowly but threateningly, and their teeth bared and growled. He quickly stepped back while Ze-chen blocked the tigers' advance. She gently patted one on the head, telling both animals that Tai-lin was her guest and she would be responsible for his visit to Heaven. The tigers stared at Tai-lin with a questioning look on their faces. Then, reluctantly, they retreated to their places at each side of the Gate, and sat down. They were quiet but warily watched as Tai-lin was following Ze-chen into Heaven.

當他們穿過南天門時,織成向泰林耳語,"進了天堂後，不管你遇到誰，都不要把你的來歷告訴對方，譬如說你從那裡來的及如何來到天堂。除了這些以外，你可以要做什麼就做什麼；不過最好仍然一直和我在一塊兒。”

While they were passing through the Gate, Ze-chen whispered to Tai-lin, "After entering the Heaven, no matter whom you meet, don't reveal your background, such as where you come from or how you came here. Other than that, you can do whatever you want, but it's better to be with me all the time."

“不要擔心這些，” 泰林被老虎的驚駭終於安定了下來，他向她擔保，“我會把你的話語記在心上的。”

"Don't worry about that." Tai-lin assured her as his breathing slowed back to the normal from his frightening confrontation with the tigers, "I'll take your words to heart."

然後他們手牽著手走進了天堂，就像一對年輕情人樣地在街道上作午後漫步。

Then they walked into Heaven, hand in hand, like young lovers taking an afternoon stroll about the street.

當泰林行走在大道上時，他很快地發現這兒的氣候和人間的不同。此時已是仲秋，可是天堂裡還是像夏末一樣地怡人，不太冷也不太熱，真是最好的天氣。

While Tai-lin was walking on the main boulevard, he soon noticed that the weather in Heaven was much different than that in the human world. Although the season was in the middle of autumn, it still felt like late summer in Heaven, the most pleasant of climate, neither too hot nor too cold.

"啊，今天的天氣真好，" 泰林說。

"Oh, the weather is so nice today," Tai-lin remarked.

"這是天堂裡的典型天氣，一年到頭永遠是這樣的。天堂裡不像人間是沒有所謂四個季節的，" 織成輕快地解釋道。

"It's the typical weather in Heaven all the year round, never changing. There are no distinctions of the so-called four seasons like those in the world of humans," Ze-chen explained pleasantly.

道路兩旁的大樹初看起來和人世間的沒有什麼不同，可是泰林再一細看，發現大樹在這兩個世界裡還是有著很大的區別的。人間的樹，有高有低，可是天堂裡的樹則是非常地整齊，每一株樹都是同樣地高低，就好像有一群訓練有素的園丁們不停地整理過似的。樹上沒有一根枯枝，地上也沒有一片落葉。

The tall trees at both sides of the road seemingly looked no different from the ones in the human world. But Tai-lin soon learned there was still a big difference between the trees in the two worlds. Trees in the human world were not all the same height, some taller and some shorter. But the ones in Heaven were all the exact same height. It looked like they were constantly well taken care of by professional gardeners. They had no dead branches and their leaves did not fall on the ground.

　　織成說天堂裡的樹是永遠不長也不會枯萎的，一旦生長在那兒，它們就永遠在那兒而且永遠是那個樣子；她告訴他她從未看到過一片黃葉除非她到人間去旅遊。

Ze-chen explained that the trees in Heaven never grew or withered. Once they were there, they would be there forever and always in the same shape. She told him that she had never seen a yellow or gold colored leaf until she had visited the human world.

　　不久，他們遇到了很多男男女女的行人，似乎每一位都是快快樂樂，好像沒有一個是愁眉苦臉的。 *"難道天堂裡真的沒有煩惱嗎？"* 泰林想。

They soon met many other travelers, male and female both. It seemed that every face wore a pleasant expression, no one with a long face or a serious manner. *"Is it true that there is simply no such thing called worry in Heaven?"* Tai-lin thought.

　　因為大家都是那麼地無拘無束，沒有一位對他們特別注意什麼，泰林也就輕鬆了下來。

As everybody was carefree, nobody paid attention to the

couple allowing Tai-lin to relax.

終於織成將泰林帶到了一座淡咖啡色的房子面前，告訴他這是她的家。泰林近前一看，驚奇地發現這棟房子都是由瑪瑙砌成的。

Finally, Ze-chen led Tai-lin to a light brown colored house and told him it was her home. Tai-lin walked toward it for a closer look and was surprised to find that the building was made totally of agate.

「你房子的建材竟是這麼貴重的寶石！」泰林驚駭莫名。

"What an expensive gemstone your house material is!" Tai-lin exclaimed, awed.

「當我申請這棟房子時，我可以選擇任何物質做我的房屋建材，」織成說。「因為我喜歡瑪瑙的顏色，所以我選擇它作為我的房子建材。假如我要鑽石作為我的房子建材，那我的房子便是由鑽石砌成的。」

"Well, I could have had any material I wanted when I applied for a house," Ze-chen said. "Because I love the color of agate, I chose it as my house material. If I had wanted diamonds, my house would have been built of diamonds."

接著她又說，「我不喜歡鑽石，可我真想不透為什麼人世間的人們對這種發光的石頭會那麼瘋狂地喜愛。"

Then, she added, "I don't like diamonds, though, and wonder why people in the human world are so crazy about such a shiny stone."

於是泰林問她黃金如何。織成回答黃金的硬度不是很好而且又太沉重了，不適合做住宅的建材，不過有些公共建築物如南天門等可還是用黃金砌成的。在天堂裡沒有建築公司，也沒有建築工人去蓋房子。當仙人需要一棟房子時，只要到政府的辦公室去申請一下。當申請者回來的時候，房子就完完整整地在那兒等著申請者了，一切就是如此地簡單，織成解釋道。

Then Tai-lin asked her how about gold. Ze-chen replied that gold was not strong enough, too weak and too heavy for building a residence. Only some public buildings such as Southern Heaven Gate were made of solid gold. In Heaven, there were no construction companies or laborers to build houses. All an immortal needed to do was to go to the government office and apply for it. When the applicant returned, the house would be waiting, complete. Everything was that simple, she explained.

進入屋來，泰林發現織成的家就像人間一棟豪華的高級住宅一樣，什麼現代化的東西都有，包括一台三十六英寸的彩色電視機，一部最新式的電腦，以及房子角落還有個小型卡拉 OK 音響舞臺。

Entering in the house, Tai-lin saw that Ze-chen had just about everything found in a luxurious house in the human world, including a 36-inch color television set, a computer of the latest style, as well as karaoke musical equipment set up on a small, raised stage in a corner.

坐定後，織成問泰林他是否餓了。他回答是的，於是她走進她的廚房，立即端出來好幾盤精美的菜餚，還有一瓶紅葡萄酒。泰林很奇怪，問她怎麼這麼快就將飯菜燒好了。她笑著回答，她不需要動手去燒，只要用手向爐灶上指點一下而已，而爐灶就立刻照她的要求把飯菜做了出來。

After their taking seats, Ze-chen asked Tai-lin if he was hungry. When he said yes, she went to her kitchen and immediately bought out several dishes of delicious food, together with a bottle of red wine. Tai-lin was amazed. He asked her how she had cooked so fast. She answered with a smile that she did not need to cook but pointed to the cooking stove and the dishes came out instantaneously as she asked.

用完了餐並喝完了那一整瓶的紅葡萄酒後，織成又用手向著飯桌一揮，所有的剩菜剩飯包括盤碗餐具等都不見了。

After they had eaten their dinner and finished the bottle of wine, Ze-chen raised her hand and waved at the dining table, and all of the food left on the plates, the dirty dishes, and the utensils disappeared.

　　"我們仙人是不喜歡做什麼洗碗工作的，" 她向驚訝的泰林嫣然一笑地說。

"We immortals do not like to do dishes," she charmingly told the astonished Tai-lin.

　　然後織成邀請泰林到客廳裡看電視，他們雙雙坐在一張泰林從未坐過的最舒適的情人座上。泰林又發現在天堂裡可以看到人間任何一個國家裡的任何電臺，真是美妙極了。

Then Ze-chen invited Tai-lin into the living room to watch TV. They sat on a comfortable love seat made of the softest material Tai-lin had ever felt. Tai-lin soon learned that they could get any TV channel from any nation in the human world. It was wonderful.

　　電視裡正在播放著一個英俊男子和兩個年輕美麗女孩的浪漫故事，好像是來自北歐一個國家，時常有接吻和擁抱等激情鏡頭出現，最後男女主角們都一件件地脫光了衣服在雙人大床上滾來滾去。他們相互親吻撫摸，當這個男子扒上一個女子的身上做愛時，另一個女子就去按摩這個女子的奶子。

The episode they watched was a very hot show, probably from a northern European nation, involving a handsome man and two pretty girls. There were many scenes of kissing and hugging. Finally, the man and women all took off their clothes, piece by piece, and rolled together on the queen-sized bed. They began kissing each other and fondling each of the other two. Finally, the man climbed on top of one girl. As they were having sex, the other girl massaged the girl's breasts.

泰林在中國從來沒有看過這類的電影，所以他對著銀光幕聚精會神地觀賞。織成緩緩地站了起來，溫柔地坐到泰林的懷中，她那白色絲質襯衫的扣子半開著，兩隻豐滿的乳房幾乎完全暴露了出來。抱著這麼一位美麗性感的半裸女孩，泰林不能控制自己而將嘴巴放在她的嘴巴上面。他的左手摟著她的腰身，右手伸進了她的上衣裡去撫摸她那豐柔的乳房，同時他和織成仍在不停地熱吻著。

Tai-lin had never seen this kind of movie in China. He was concentrating on the screen when Ze-chen slowly stood up, then, gently sat on his lap. Her white silk shirt was half open and almost totally exposed her two lush breasts. Holding such a pretty, sexy, and half-naked girl in his arms, Tai-lin could not help but put his mouth on hers. While using his left hand to hug her waist, he slipped his right hand into her shirt to caress her plump breasts, and he and Ze-chen continued warmly kissing each other.

這是泰林有生以來第一次親吻一個女人的嘴巴及第一次撫摸女人的乳房。*"啊，真是妙極了！"*

It was Tai-lin's first time kissing a woman's mouth and

touching a woman's breasts. *Oh, it is great!*

　　他很驚訝織成的乳房怎麼這麼樣地柔軟。她將她襯衫上的其餘釦子都解開了，把她的襯衫從她的肩膀上滑落了下去。織成愉快地呻吟著，一邊將泰林的頭按向她的前胸，於是，他將她的一隻乳頭含在口中，像一個飢餓嬰兒吸奶一樣地吸著。

He was surprised at how soft Ze-chen's breasts were. He unbuttoned the rest of her blouse and slipped it off her shoulders. Ze-chen moaned with pleasure as she pulled Tai-lin's head down to her chest and he took one of her breasts in his mouth and began sucking it like a hungry infant.

　　然後，織成站了起來，用手將泰林拉入她的臥房，幫他將他的衣服脫光了，接著又風情萬種地把她自己的其餘衣服也脫了下來。她立刻看到了泰林的激昂，就像剛才他們在電視上所看到的那個男子的一模一樣。

After that, Ze-chen stood up, took Tai-lin by a hand and led him into her bedroom. She helped him undress then seductively removed the rest of her clothes. She immediately saw Tai-lin's arousal, like the man's on the television show they had watched.

　　泰林在中國和他的女友蘋蘋交往多年，可是，因為他們兩人都很保守，他們從來沒有做過超越握手以上的肢體接觸。有一次，他想擁抱一下他的女友，她立刻退後警告他在他們結婚前是不可以再有這種舉動的。

Tai-lin had dated his girlfriend, Pin-pin, in China for several years, but they both were very conservative and physically had never gone beyond a handshake. Once he tried to hug his girl, and she immediately retreated and warned him not to try it again before they were married.

現在，泰林和織成赤裸裸地躺在一張雙人床上擁抱著滾來滾去，和剛才電視上的男女主角一模一樣。於一連串的親吻和撫摸後，她引導他進入了她的身體，他們做愛了。泰林終於領略到了一個男人和一個女人混爲一體時的舒暢，在這種銷魂的時刻，泰林完全忘記了他在人間的一切煩惱，只有緊緊地抱著懷中這個性感赤裸還在呻吟著的美麗仙女。

Now Tai-lin and Ze-chen, rolling on a queen-sized bed, totally naked, just like the man and women on the TV screen. After much kissing and fondling, she guided him inside of her and they made love, which made Tai-lin finally realized how wonderful it was when a man and a woman became one. At this moment of ecstasy Tai-lin forgot all about his problems in the human world, but pulling the sexy, naked, beautiful fairy tightly to him while she was moaning.

因爲這是泰林的第一次性行爲，即使做完了愛，他仍感到無比的興奮。當織成睡熟了後，這股興奮依然使他無法成眠。眼睛張著，他輕撫著睡在身旁的這個赤裸美女，自己卻一點兒睡意也沒有，可他那在人間的顛簸一生，就好像是一部電影裡的故事情節一樣，一幕一幕地呈現在他的腦海中了。

It was Tai-lin's first sexual experience. Even after it was over, the fantastic feeling he had experienced kept him awake long after Ze-chen fell asleep. With his eyes open, he cuddled the naked sleeping beauty, but he could not sleep. His own unpleasant life in the human world appeared in his brain like movie scenario, repeating one after the other.

第二章　Chapter Two

蔡泰林是中國四川省一個遍辟地區的青年男子。高中畢業後，因為無法升入大學，乃和其他無力升學的高中畢業生一樣，只想找到一個工作，能有固定的收入，將來也可以娶妻生子成家立業。因為他有一個親戚，他母親的弟弟，是四川省第二人口最多的都市成都市內一家規模很大名叫"康復成衣工廠"裡的副總經理，所以他很快地找到了一個職位，在這家工廠裡做個設計師助理。他對這個工作和工作環境非常滿意，因而工作得也就特別認真努力。一年後，他就升任為一個正式設計師，每月的薪金也由八百元調整為一千一百元。

Tai-lin Cai was a high school graduate in a remote area in the Province of Si-chuan, China. Like every Chinese high school graduate who could not go to college, he wanted to find a job making a steady income and eventually marry a young woman who would bear a child, making a family of their own. He received help from a relative, his mother's younger brother who was an assistant general manager of Comfort Garment Factory, a large business in Chen-du, the second most populous city in the Province of Si-chuan. Tai-lin was hired as a designer's assistant. He was very satisfied with the job and the working atmosphere and worked diligently. A year later, he was promoted to the position of designer and his monthly salary was raised from eight hundred yuans to one thousand and one hundred yuans.

　　服裝設計部共有四十多名工作人員，一個主任，是男性，三個副主任，兩個男性，一個女性。他們都在四十上下，已有家室。大家都明瞭泰林是他們副總經理的外甥，因此對他就特別地多方照顧。

There were more than forty workers in the design department including one director and three assistant directors. The director and two assistant directors were men while the other assistant director was a woman. They were all around forties, married with their own families. When they realized that Tai-lin was their assistant general manager's nephew, they were especially nice to him.

　　就在泰林升任為正式設計師後不久，設計部裡來了另一位女性同事，是個十七八歲的女孩，人長得很美，名叫林蘋蘋。她是個新人，也是部裡職位最低的僱員，助理辦事員，聽命於設計師及保管設計師所設計的各種圖樣。

Soon after Tai-lin was promoted to the position of designer, another female was hired to work in the design department. She was a pretty girl in her late teens named Pin-pin Lin. She was the department's new assistant clerk, the department's lowest position. She took orders from the designers and kept the design records for them.

慢慢地，大家都知道了蘋蘋來自一個貧窮的人家。她的父母親都失業很久了，他們原來在一家國營企業裡工作，因為很多家國營企業多年來一直賠本，所以當中國政府實行改革開放政策後，乃把這些國營企業關閉，或者乾脆賣給私人企業，於是千萬個工作人員便都失業了。蘋蘋的父母親就是這類失業人員。

It gradually became known that Pin-pin was from a poor family. Her parents had been unemployed for a long time. They had worked in a state enterprise but many state enterprises were under bad management and loaded with debts. When China turned to its open policy, those state enterprises were ordered to close doors or be sold to private organizations. Hundreds of thousands of people lost their jobs. Pin-pin's parents were two of those people.

　　雖然這類失業人員每人每月都可以從政府中領到四百元的生活費用，可是對於一個三口之家來說，即使是維持最底的生活水準仍是不夠的。因此，這對夫婦還必須打些零工去賺個另外數百元方可維生。在這種情況下，蘋蘋又根本不喜歡讀書，她便從中學裡申請退學，在這家成衣工廠中找到了一個工作，每月領取五百六十元的工資，幫助父母應付各種家庭開支。所以蘋蘋很節省，她從不浪費所賺來的一文錢。

Although each of those people who lost their jobs received four hundred yuans a month from the government as a kind of benefit to survive on, it was not enough to make a simple living for a family of three. Therefore, Pin-pin's parents had to find to work as temporary laborers to earn a few hundred yuans of extra income each month. Under such circumstances, and since she was never fond of studying, Pin-pin dropped out of high school and found her job with the garment factory. She made five hundred and sixty yuans a month to help her parents pay the living expenses. Therefore, she was very frugal, never wasting one penny she earned.

　　蘋蘋是個天生的美女。不久，所有設計部裡的男性工作人員都注意到了這個新來的漂亮女孩。泰林是設計部裡幾個少數尚未成婚的男性員工，更重要的是他長得非常英俊。很自然地，泰林也贏得了蘋蘋的注意。可是，這兩個年輕人都很保守，雖然他們白天一起工作，下班後他們卻從不往來。

Pin-pin was a born beauty. Soon, all the male employees in

the design department paid attention to the newly hired pretty girl. Tai-lin was one of the few male employees in the department who were still single, and most importantly, he was very handsome. So it seemed natural that Tai-lin caught the eyes of Pin-pin as well. But both of the two young people were very conservative. Although they worked together in the daytime, there were no private meetings between them after office hours.

蘋蘋的工作之一是保管設計師所設計的圖樣。一天,當蘋蘋無法找到一個脾氣很壞的設計師在一個星期前所設計的圖樣時,他向蘋蘋大聲吼叫,責備她亂放到別處去了。指責使得她感到羞愧,眼淚包在眼眶裡可她不敢在公共場所大聲哭出來。

One of Pin-pin's jobs was to keep the records of the designers' creations. One day, when Pin-pin could not find a bad tempered designer's record from the week before, he yelled at her, blaming her for misplacing it. His accusation made her feel ashamed. But she dared not cry in public though she had tears in her eyes.

泰林湊巧經過,聽到了蘋蘋和設計師的對話,他主動上去幫助蘋蘋。經過他的幫助,終於找出了檔案中的老圖樣。因為每個人都知道泰林在工廠裡有個強有力的親戚,而他自己也工作得很勤奮比同一部門裡的其他工作人員都努力,這個設計師也就不再責備蘋蘋便走開了。

Tai-lin happened to pass by and overheard the exchange of words between Pin-pin and the designer. He voluntarily gave Pin-pin a hand. With his help, the file of the old design was finally found. Because everybody knew that Tai-lin had a powerful relative in the factory and he himself worked harder than all the other workers in the department, the designer stopped blaming Pin-pin and walked away.

"真感激你的好心幫助，" 蘋蘋紅著臉含著一眶感激的淚水向泰林低語。

"Thank you for your kind help," Pin-pin whispered to Tai-pin. She blushed with appreciative tears in her eyes.

"沒有什麼啦，蘋蘋。我們是同事，應該相互幫助的，" 泰林輕聲地說。

"That's all right, Pin-pin. As colleagues, we should help each other," Tai-lin said softly.

自從這次事件後，只要這兩個年輕人在走道上遇見了，如果沒有其他的人在場，他們定會聊上一兩句話，可是，他們兩人中任何一人仍是沒有勇氣提出一個約會。

After that incident, the two young people often exchanged a few words whenever they met in the lobby if nobody else was present. Still neither of them had the courage to ask the other for a date.

　　雖然他們沒有要求約會，可他們在每天午飯後時常坐在飯廳的一角相聚。當他們還有十或十五分鐘的休息時間才回去工作時，他們就會開始多聊聊。對於他們來說，能夠每天見個面談幾句話也就心滿意足了，這兩個年輕人把他們的秘密的愛深藏在他們的心裡。

Although they did not ask for a date, they often sat together after lunch at a corner of the dining room to talk during the last ten or fifteen minutes of break before they had to go back to work. It seemed that being able to see each other and have a chance to speak every day was very satisfied for the two young people who kept their secret love in their hearts.

　　一天，蘋蘋沒有來上班，第二天她也沒有來。這使得泰林非常擔心；然而他沒有勇氣去問她的工頭，一個中年婦人，設計部裡的資深雇員，她怎麼了或為什麼。這個婦人很機靈，她早已發現了泰林和蘋蘋之間的秘密愛情，所以在午飯後休息的時間，她走近了泰林，悄悄地遞給他一張紙條，告訴他蘋蘋的母親病重。那就是為什麼她要請三天假。在這張字條上還有蘋蘋家的地址，她建議泰林去拜訪蘋蘋和她的家人。

One day, Pin-pin was not at work, nor did the next day. Tai-lin became worried; yet he did not have the courage to ask her boss, a middle-aged woman, a senior clerk in the department, why Pin-pin was absent. But the woman was astute and had already noticed the secret love developing between Tai-lin and Pin-pin. So after lunch during the break time, she approached Tai-lin and quietly handed him a note telling him that Pin-pin's mother was seriously ill. That was the reason why she had asked for three days off. Also on the note was Pin-pin's address. The senior clerk suggested that Tai-lin pay her and her family a visit.

　　泰林含羞地謝了這個婦人。下班後，他到那張字條上所寫的地址給予蘋蘋一個驚喜的拜訪。他帶了一包罐頭食物作為禮品。蘋蘋母親的病已經大為見好了，這對老夫婦和蘋蘋一樣地高興來接待泰林，這個剛病癒的婦人更是不停地訊問泰林的家庭情況。

Tai-lin shyly thanked the woman. After work, he went to the place indicated on the note to pay Pin-pin a surprise visit. He took a package of canned food as a gift. Pin-pin's mother was much improved, and she, Pin-pin's father and Pin-pin gave Tai-lin a joyful welcome. The newly recovered woman further kept inquiring about Tai-lin's family.

　　泰林的父母在他讀初中的時候就過世了，他沒有兄弟姐妹，他是被他父親的哥哥他的大伯和大伯母帶養大的。泰林高中畢業找到了這個成衣廠工作後，他就搬出了伯父母的家獨立生活了。他在距離工廠不遠處租了一個小公寓住著。

Both of Tai-lin's parents had died when he was in junior

high school, and he had no brothers or sisters. He was brought up by his uncle, his father's elder brother, and his uncle's wife. After Tai-lin graduated from senior high school and found the job at the garment factory, he moved out of his uncle and aunt's home and became independent. He rented a small apartment not too far from the factory.

當泰林向她的家人告別時，蘋蘋陪著他到外面巷子裡，這兩個年輕人第一次終於有了個單獨談話的機會，可是他們的談話中仍然沒有個愛字。

When Tai-lin said good-bye to her family, Pin-pin accompanied him outside to the alley where the two young people finally had an opportunity to talk privately. Yet, there were still no actual words of love in their conversation.

從此後，泰林和蘋蘋就自認為是情侶了。星期天，當他們不去工廠工作時，他就會邀請她和他一道去看場電影或去什麼娛樂場所。慢慢地全設計部裡的同事們都知道他們相愛了，每個人都認為如果他們結婚了那將是一對理想伴侶。因為泰林的關係，那個脾氣不好曾經向蘋蘋吼叫過的設計師即使蘋蘋又犯了錯誤也不再向她吼叫了。

From that time on, Tai-lin and Pin-pin considered them lovers. On Sundays, their day off from work, they would see a movie or go to some entertainment together. Gradually, the whole design department came to understand their love and they all agreed that they would make a perfect couple if they married. Because of Tai-lin, the quick-tempered designer who had yelled at Pin-pin before never raised his voice to her again, even when she made another mistake.

泰林和蘋蘋除了星期天以外每天中午都在同一張桌子上吃飯，而工廠裡的同事們也視爲當然。似乎是他們所要等待的就是接到泰林和蘋蘋的結婚喜帖請他們去參加婚禮了。

Now Tai-lin and Pin-pin ate lunch at the same table every weekday and every co-worker in the factory accepted it as natural. It seemed that all they were waiting for was Tai-lin and Pin-pin's invitation asking them to attend their wedding ceremony.

十月一日是中國國慶日。在一九四九年的這一天，已過世的中國共產黨國家主席毛澤東公開向全世界宣佈中華人民共和國的成立，他們把蔣介石的國民黨政府趕去了臺灣佔據了整個中國大陸。每年的今日，全中國各地都會舉辦各式各樣的娛樂活動來慶祝這個偉大的節日。

October 1 was the Chinese National Holiday. On this day in 1949, the late Chinese communist government chairman, Mao Zedong, publicly announced to the world the establishment of the People's Republic of China, after driving away the Chiang Kai-shek's Nationalist Chinese government to Taiwan and occupying the whole China mainland. On this day every year, the whole nation of China celebrates the great holiday with various joyous activities.

　　康復成衣工廠舉辦了一個包含很多慶祝活動的茶會。選舉一位年度模範員工是茶會中一個重要的節目。果如大家所預料到的，泰林被選中了，總經理在數千名員工面前公開宣佈蔡泰林為年度的模範員工。泰林除了獲得三百元的獎金外，還被提升為設計部副主任，因為一位副主任被調往另一個部門去了。

Comfort Garment Factory held a tea party with many celebration programs on that day. Choosing an employee of the year became a big event at the party. As everybody expected, Tai-lin Cai's name was declared by the general manager in front of several thousand employees to be the employee of the year. Tai-lin was awarded three hundred yuans along with a promotion to assistant director of the design department, while one assistant director was transferred to another department.

　　這就是說泰林的月薪將從一千一百元增加為一千五百元，而蘋蘋的薪資仍然是每個月不到六百元。

It meant that Tai-lin's monthly salary would be raised from one thousand and one hundred yuans to one thousand and five hundred yuans, while Pin-pin's was still less than six hundred yuans a month.

散會後，泰林邀請蘋蘋在成都市一家高級飯店裡吃晚飯，泰林叫了很多道她喜愛的菜餚，並且又叫了一小瓶葡萄酒。用餐中，泰林告訴蘋蘋等他再升一級變成部主任時，他的月薪便會增加爲一千九百元，足夠維持一個家了，然後他就會要求她嫁給他，而他們也就會有一個舒適的生活。

After the party, Tai-lin invited Pin-pin to have supper with him at one of the finest restaurants in Chen-du. Tai-lin ordered many of her favorable dishes along with a small bottle of wine. During the meal, Tai-lin told Pin-pin that when he was promoted one more step to become the department director, he would be making one thousand and nine hundred yuans a month, big enough to support a family, then he would ask her to marry him, and they would have a comfortable life.

泰林握著她的手，蘋蘋紅著臉，一語不發地含羞點了下頭。飯後，泰林步行送她到汽車站。看附近沒有其他乘客，在這溫柔的月光下，泰林想擁抱她一下。出乎意料，她突然退後幾步，鄭重地告訴他，在他們結婚以前，除了握手以外，他不可以接觸她的身體。

While Tai-lin held Pin-pin's hand, she blushed, nodded with a shy smile without saying a word. After the meal, Tai-lin walked her to a bus station. As no other travelers were in sight, under the soft moonlight, Tai-lin tried to hug her. Unexpectedly, she quickly retreated a few steps. She told him in a serious manner that she would not let him touch her body except shaking-hands before their marriage.

蘋蘋是這麼一個保守的女孩！泰林不但不生氣，反而立刻向她道歉，並向她保證，他會把她的話語記在心中，在結婚前再也不會有此企圖了。

Pin-pin was such a conservative girl! Instead of being unhappy, Tai-lin quickly apologized to her and assured her that he would take her words to heart and never try again before they married.

現在，泰林工作比以前更加努力了，希望能夠再升一級，然後和他的戀人蘋蘋結婚。但是，天下的事情並不是如他所企盼地那樣進行。

Now, Tai-lin worked even harder than before, hoping for another promotion so he would marry his sweetheart, Pin-pin. But, things did not go as well as he expected.

當工廠的經理部門發現他們的成衣在國內市場上的銷路日趨艱難時，乃決定將他們的產品銷售到海外，特別是美國和歐洲的市場。於是一個曾在美國讀過一年書的青年便被聘僱為新成立的外銷部主任，同時挑選了八個懂點英文的員工做他的助手。

As the sales of the factory's garments in the domestic market had fallen for several years, the management of factory decided to export their products overseas, particularly to the markets in the United States and Europe. A young man who had received one year of education in the United States was hired as the director of newly established export department overseeing eight selected employees who understood some simple English.

由於外銷部門人員的薪金比生產部門的人員高得很多，一時間學習英文便突然成了一種風氣，而去美國學習更變成了每一個年輕工作人員的夢想，蘋蘋就是其中之一位；可是泰林不是的。

Because the salaries of the employees in the export department were much higher than the workers in the producing departments, learning English suddenly became fashionable and going to the United States to study turned out to be every young worker's dream. Pin-pin was one of those dreamers, but Tai-lin was not.

蘋蘋於放工後，便到街上一家英文夜校裡去補習英文，可是泰林便不去。他告訴她，由於他們兩人的學力背景不強，想把英文學好到美國去深造是非常地困難，因此他寧願留在這個他出生及住了一輩子的地方。換言之，他是個偏重實際而不是個夢想者。

After work, Pin-pin began to attend night school class in downtown to learn English, but Tai-lin did not. He told her that since their educational background was not strong it would be very difficult for them to improve their English well enough to go to the United States for advanced studies. He would rather stay in the country where he was born and had lived all of his life. In other words, he was much more practical than a dreamer.

　　他說在事業上他已經有了一個好的開始了，他要朝著這個方向去努力升到一個部門主管，賺到足夠的收入可以舒服地成家。他告訴她他們的苦難的國家已經終於找到了一個正確的方向去前進，他們的國家領導人已經為人民訂下了一個光明的藍圖，他們為什麼不跟隨著國家領導人的指示去做呢？到美國去讀書對於一些大學畢業的人來說可能是件好事，可對於一些如他和蘋蘋一樣的人來說是很不適合的，泰林分析道。

　　He said that since he had already had a good beginning on a career, he wanted to work toward his goal of becoming a department head making enough money to support a family in comfort. He told her that their suffering country had finally found the right way of progressing, and their national leaders had drawn a bright blueprint for their people to follow. Why shouldn't they act in accordance with the national leaders' directions? Going to America to study might be appropriate for some people like college graduates, but not for the people like him and Pin-pin, Tai-lin reasoned.

　　他要她放棄去美國的念頭，就停留在中國。可是她不同意，她說根據她所聽到的美國是當今世界上最富裕的國家，在那裡人們有最好的機會去賺大錢，享受豪華的人生。「如果你真的愛我，」她對他說，「你應該去做像我現在所做的去讀英文，然後我們一起去美國，在那兒結婚，而不要在中國成立家庭。」

Tai-lin advised Pin-pin to drop the idea of going to America and to stay in China instead. But Pin-pin did not agree. She said as much as she had heard about the United States, it was the richest country in the world where people had the best chances to make great amount of money and enjoy the luxurious life. "If you really love me," she said to him, "you should study English like what I'm doing now, then we'll go to America together and get married there instead of starting a family here in China."

　　每次他們討論他們的前途時總是如此地不歡而別。蘋蘋繼續去夜校讀英文，而泰林則選擇儘可能去加班好多賺些錢，留著結婚時花費及婚後用途。他們仍然交往，一同去看電影或去到那些年輕情侶們時常去的地方遊玩。每次分手時，他們便會熱情地握手道別，不過從未超越此一防線，完全遵守蘋蘋的要求及泰林的承諾。

　　Their discussion about their future always ended in such unhappiness. Pin-pin kept studying English at a night school while Tai-lin chose to work overtime as much as possible in order to make more money for their wedding use and life after that. They still dated, going to a movie or some other places where most of the young lovers often went. They shook hands in affection every time they said good- bye, but never went beyond that line, as Pin-pin wanted and Tai-lin had promised.

雖然他們在讀英文及去美國的觀念上有不同的分歧，兩個戀愛中人的日子仍然在愉快中度過一直到有一天，蘋蘋的一個女性朋友帶來了另一位也是女性的朋友。這個女人和蘋蘋一樣也夢想去美國，可她終於達成了她的願望，停留那裡差不多兩年半光景。。

Despite their difference of opinions about studying English and going to America, time went by pleasantly for the two lovers until one day one of Pin-pin's girlfriends brought in another young woman. Like Pin-pin, the woman had also dreamed of going to America and she had finally made it, staying there for about two and half years.

沒有人知道她是如何獲得簽証抑或根本沒有不過是走非法途徑的進入美國的。總之，當她回到中國時，她的口袋裡多了兩萬多美元。一美元在那時相當八元人民幣，比起那些像蘋蘋一樣每個月只賺五、六百元的工作人員來說，這個年輕女人便成了富婆了。很自然地，這個富裕女人的案例給予蘋蘋的印象深刻之至。

No one knew how she got a visa or if she perhaps never had one but had entered America through an illegal way.

Regardless, when she returned to China, she had more than twenty thousand dollars in American currency in her pocket. As one US dollar was then equivalent to eight Chinese yuans, the young woman suddenly became a wealthy woman, compared to the five-or-six-hundred-yuans-a-month workers like Pin-pin. Naturally, the wealthy woman's case impressed Pin-pin very much.

　　不管蘋蘋如何努力，這個女人就是不願意說出她是怎樣進入美國的。蘋蘋終於放棄了，繼續努力去讀她的英文。她發誓當機會到了時，她也會去美國的。

No matter how hard Pin-pin tried to learn how the woman had entered the United States, the woman would not tell her. Finally, Pin-pin gave up, but concentrated more intensely on her English studies, vowing that she, too, would go to America when the chance presented itself.

　　也許因為泰林的工作表現的確出色，也許因為在經理部門他有個強有力的舅舅，當泰林的部門主管升級了後，泰林便被命令去接替他的職位成為部門主任。這也就是說泰林的每月薪金也從一千五百元調整為一千九百元了。

Maybe because Tai-lin's performance was indeed excellent, or maybe because he had an uncle in a powerful management position, when Tai-lin's department head was promoted, Tai-lin was also promoted to take over as the department director. It meant that Tai-lin's salary jumped from one thousand and five hundred yuans to one thousand and nine hundred yuans a month.

泰林非常興奮，並不光是因爲升級，而是因爲他可以賺足夠的錢來養家活口去和蘋蘋結婚了

Tai-lin was elated, not simply because of his promotion, but because he would earn enough money to support a family after he married Pin-pin.

他興高采烈地邀請蘋蘋在下班後與他共進晚餐及告訴她這個興奮的消息。同時，他正式向她求婚要她嫁給他。

He excitedly invited Pin-pin to have supper after work and told her the happy news. Meanwhile, he formally courted her to marry him.

完全出乎泰林的意料之外，蘋蘋連考慮也沒有就立刻拒絕他的求婚。理由很簡單，她夢想去美國。「我已經告訴過你一百次了，我不要和你在中國結婚。如果你真的愛我，讓我們去美國，我們在那兒結婚，」蘋蘋以絲毫不容妥協的語氣告訴他。

Totally unexpected by Tai-lin, his courtship was turned down by Pin-pin immediately without consideration. Her reason was simple that she dreamed of going to the United States. "I have told you a hundred times. I don't want to marry you in

China. If you really love me, let us go to America and marry there," Pin-pin told him in a way that could not be compromised.

蘋蘋的拒絕徹底粉碎了泰林的夢想，他整整一夜無法成眠。接著的三天是個長假日，泰林決定去到附近的峨嵋山上去好好地思考他的下一步該怎麼走，是完全放棄蘋蘋還是跟隨著她去讀英文，和她一起去美國。

Pin-pin's rejection crushed Tai-lin's dream so deeply that he did not sleep well that night. Since the next three days were a long holiday away from work, Tai-lin decided to go up to the nearby E-Mei Mountain to be alone and to think through what he should do next - either sever his relationship with Pin-pin totally, or also study English and go with her to the United States.

帶著一包熟食及飲料，泰林在天一亮便上山了，露水仍然灑在地上，太陽也仍然躲在雲霧後面。峨嵋山是中國十大高山之一，山上有很多神秘的美景。從峨嵋山上望日出在夏季的涼爽早晨經常吸引很多的人。可是在這仲秋季節，沒有人們出現。

With a package of cooked food and drinks, Tai-lin went up the mountain in a very early morning as dew still covered the ground and the clouds hid the sun. E-Mei Mountain was one of the ten highest mountains in China with many interesting myths attached to it. Watching a sunrise from E-Mei Mountain always attracted many people in the coolness of summer mornings, but now in this middle of autumn, few people showed up.

泰林徘徊在一處峭壁，那是個遙望日出的最佳地點，可他對於欣賞這大自然的美景一點兒興趣也沒有，卻不停地自言自語著我的下一步應該如何走。

Tai-lin lingered by a cliff, the best spot from where to watch the sunrise. But his interest was not in viewing the natural beauty that surrounded him, but kept murmuring, asking what he should do next.

他深愛蘋蘋已經有好幾年了，自從她到到工廠工作後不久他就愛上了她。可是，他不同意她去美國的夢想，然而他無法使她改變她的想法。他沒有興趣去讀英文，也沒有意願去到任何一個外國。多少年來，他唯一的希望是能夠再升一級成為部門的主任，那麼，他的薪金就會提升到足夠維持一個舒適的家庭了。現在他終於達成了他的願望，可是她拒絕了他的求婚。

He had fallen deeply in love with Pin-pin for several years soon after she started to work in the factory. But he did not agree to her dream of going to the United States; meanwhile, he could not make her change her mind, either. He was not interested in studying English and had no desire to go to any foreign nation whatsoever. For years, all he had wished for was to be promoted to the head of his department so his salary would be raised high enough for him to support a family comfortably. Now that he finally had what he had wished, but Pin-pin rejected his courtship.

　　不，那也並不完全是對的。她並不是完全拒絕他的求婚，不過希望能在美國結婚而不是在中國。他和蘋蘋一樣也聽到過很多關於美國的美好故事，他明瞭對於中國大學畢業生們來說，美國可能是個進修的好地方。不過，對於他和蘋蘋一類中學程度的人來說，絕對不是個適宜的地方。但是，蘋蘋已經被這個去美國的想法所迷惑了。泰林真不知道如何是好。對於他來說，這最困難的事情是他不願意放棄她，因為他已經深深地明瞭在往後的日子裡，如果沒有了她他是無論如何也不會快樂起來的。

　　No, that wasn't quite correct. She did not totally turn down his courtship but insisted on getting married in the United States instead of China. Like Pin-pin, Tai-lin had also heard many positive stories about America. He understood that it might be a good place for the Chinese college graduates to do advanced studies. Definitely, though, he believed it was not a place for the high school level students like Pin-pin and him. But Pin-pin had been so bewitched by the idea of going to the United States that Tai-lin was confused. Of course, the most difficult thing for him to do would be to give her up. He deeply realized that he would not live happily without her in the days ahead if he did so.

"我真的不明瞭你為什麼不去欣賞這麼美麗的日出，卻在不斷地去憂愁個什麼事情？"一個亮麗清脆而又熱情的女性聲音突然問道。

"I'm confused why don't you enjoy such a beautiful sunrise but keep worrying about something instead?" a clear, crisp, sultry feminine voice suddenly asked.

轉過頭來，泰林驚訝地發現一位絕色年輕女子站在他的旁邊，而他連她如何來到竟然毫無感覺。

Startled, Tai-lin turned around and he was surprised to see a young lady of rare beauty standing nearby, while he had not noticed her arrival.

"你是誰？"泰林匆促地問道。

"Who are you?" Tai-lin hurriedly asked.

"我是仙女，"女子輕柔地回答。

"I'm a fairy," the girl answered softly.

"你的意思是說你不是一般的女子，而是從天堂裡來的？"泰林重複地以極不信任的態度又問。

"You mean you are not an ordinary woman, but one who comes from Heaven?" Tai-lin asked in extreme disbelief.

　　"是的，我是從天堂上來的，" 女孩嫣然一笑地對著他說。

　　"Yes, I am from Heaven," the girl answered and smiled sweetly at him.

　　面對著這個女孩還不到兩呎，泰林必須承認她的美麗是超越世間的任何一個美女，是一種飄逸絕塵沒有一點像一般女子所用的人工裝扮的美。

　　Facing the girl from a distance of less than two feet, Tai-lin admitted that her beauty was far surpassed that of any ordinary woman. She possessed a kind of pure natural beauty that did not need the enhancement of make-up so many women used.

　　"如果你真的是一位仙女，" 泰林仍然非常懷疑地說，"我可以告訴你我的故事請你給我個忠告。"

　　"If you are really a fairy," Tai-lin said, his tone still doubtful, "I'll tell you my story and ask for your advice."

　　"坐下告訴我吧，" 女子指著泰林前面的一張很大的咖啡色皮沙發說，她自己也坐在另一張面向著他的沙發上。

　　"Have a seat and tell me." The lady pointed to a large brown leather sofa that had appeared in front of him, and she herself took another one facing him.

"你怎麼可以把這麼苯重的傢俱搬上山來了？" 泰林
大為驚駭。

"How could you move such heavy furniture up the
mountain?" Tai-lin was shocked at what he saw.

"我告訴過你我是一個仙女。一個仙女能做任何她所要
做的事情，" 她安靜地回答。

"I told you I am a fairy. A fairy can do anything she
wants," she answered calmly.

在這種不尋常的情況下，泰林也只好坐上了沙發，把他
在人間所發生的不愉快愛情故事一五一十儘可能地都告訴了
這個自稱仙女的年輕美麗女子。

Under such an unusual circumstance, Tai-lin lowed
himself to the sofa and told the young pretty, self-declared fairy,
his bitter love story as much as he could.

"老實說，對於凡人間的事情我並不是太瞭解。你也許
需要跟我到天堂裡去散散心。" 女子聽了泰林的故事後告訴
他，"這可能是你唯一的方法使你忘記在人間所遭遇到的所
有煩惱。"

After listening to Tai-lin's story, she told him, "Honestly, I
don't know much about the mortal affairs. But perhaps you
might need to go to Heaven with me for a while to forget all of
your earthly worries. Maybe this is the only way you can get rid

of the torture you are suffering in the world of humans."

"可是，我如何能去呢？" 泰林問道，這時候他已經相信這個女子絕不是個一般的女人了。

"But, how can I go?" Tai-lin asked, believing now that the girl was truly not an ordinary woman.

"很容易，" 女孩子說，"只要抓住我的手，閉上你的眼睛，我就可以帶你去到那兒了。"

"Very simple," the girl said, "just hold my hand, close your eyes and I'll take you there."

第三章　Chapter Three

現在泰林真的到了天堂，而且還在不久前和這個名叫織成的美麗的仙女做了愛。這一切的一切發生得太突然了，好得簡直不能使他相信。

Now Tai-lin was indeed in Heaven and had made love to the beautiful fairy named Ze-chen a little while ago. Everything had happened so suddenly and was indeed too good for him to believe.

第二天早上，當泰林醒來後，織成早已起身穿好衣服了。

When Tai-lin woke up in the morning, Ze-chen had already dressed.

和前天晚上的晚餐一樣，她用神通準備了一個美國式的早餐，有火腿、煎蛋、烤麵包及咖啡，兩套銀製的刀叉和調羹都已放在桌上。

Like with the supper of the night before, Ze-chen used her supernatural power to prepare an American style breakfast of ham, pan-fried eggs, toast and coffee. Two sets of silver forks, knives, and spoons were placed on the table.

"我相信你可能從來沒有吃過美國飯，"當他們就位時，她對他說。

"I would believe you might have never eaten an American meal," she said to him while they were taking seats at the dining table.

於是，她教他如何用刀去切肉用叉子將食物撿起來。當他用叉子將一小塊火腿送進口中後，他告訴她，"味道還真不壞呢，雖然和中國菜是完全地不同。"

Then she taught him how to use a knife to cut the meat and use a fork to pick up the food. After he used a fork to put a small piece of ham into his mouth, he told her, "It doesn't tastes too bad at all, although it is totally different from the Chinese food."

臉上掛著微笑，她說，"明天早上，我將為你準備個法國式的早餐。"

With a smile on her face, she said, "I'm going to prepare a French style of breakfast for you tomorrow morning."

泰林難以相信他的耳朵，他還要和這個迷人的織成至少再共度一個良宵。*她還會和我再做一次愛嗎？*他興奮地想著。

Tai-lin couldn't believe his ears. He was going to have at least one more night with the enchanting Ze-chen. *Would she allow me to make love to her again?* He wondered excitedly.

飯後，織成帶泰林去逛一處很大的購貨中心。購貨中心看起來和人間的幾乎沒有兩樣，這裡有來自人間各國的各種貨品。終於泰林發現了一個最大的不同，那就是這兒的每一家商店裡都沒有售貨人員，也沒有收銀機。

After the meal, Ze-chen took Tai-lin to visit a huge shopping center. The center looked no different from the ones in the world of humans, with various kinds of merchandise from all nations on the earth. But soon Tai-lin found a big difference that there were no sales people or cashiers in any of the stores.

"怎麼每一家商店裡都沒有收銀機？"泰林問道。

"How come there are no cashiers in each store?" Tai-lin asked.

"在天堂裡根本沒有所謂叫錢的東西，"織成解釋，"我們還要售貨員和收銀機做什麼？"

"There is no such thing called money in Heaven," Ze-chen explained. "What do we need sales people and cashiers for?"

因爲每一位"顧客"都拿著個大袋子，裡面裝滿了他們所需要的東西，泰林也提著個小袋子。當他們經過一家珠寶店時，他將鑽石戒指及鑽石項鏈儘可能地把他的袋子裝得滿滿地。

As every "customer" carried a large bag filled with the items they needed, Tai-lin carried a small bag in his hand. While they passed through a jewelry shop, he filled up his bag with as many diamond rings and necklaces as he could.

織成笑道，"人們真是太傻了，他們怎麼會對這些發光而又難看的東西有興趣？"

Ze-chen laughed, "The humans are indeed very foolish. How could they be interested in those ugly shining items?"

數小時後，泰林告訴她他的肚子餓了，織成乃帶他到一家金碧輝煌的飯店。他要了三道海鮮都是龍蝦和蝦子一類的食物，可織成只吃了一小碗青菜湯。和剛才在購貨中心一樣，他們也沒有付飯錢。

Several hours later, when Tai-lin told her he was little hungry, Ze-chen took him to a fancy restaurant. He ordered three dishes of seafood all made with lobsters and shrimps while she only ate a small bowl of vegetable soup. As with the merchandise in the shopping center, they did not pay for their meals.

　　午飯後，織成又帶著泰林遊逛了很多有趣的地方。他發現除了醫院和醫生診所外，人世間所有的行業天堂裡面都有了。

After lunch, Ze-chen showed Tai-lin around in many interesting places. He found just about all kinds of human business in Heaven except hospitals and medical clinics.

　　當他向織成提到這點時，她說，"因為我們神仙是從不生病的，那我們還要這些做什麼？"

When he mentioned this to Ze-chen, she said, "Because we, immortals, never become sick. What do we need those places for?"

　　然後她又接著說，"這也是為什麼你在天堂裡看不到殯儀館的原因，因為我們神仙是永遠不會死亡的。"

Then she added, "That is also the reason why you will never find a funeral home here in Heaven because we immortals do not die."

　　泰林困惑了，"如果是這樣的話，那麼天堂裡的人口不是年年急速增加，而這個世界便會擁擠不堪了。"

Tai-lin was confused, "If that is so, the population in

Heaven must be growing sharply every year and making this world very crowded."

　　"那怎麼可能呢？"織成笑了，"我們仙女是不生育的。"

"How could it happen?" Ze-chen smiled, "We fairies do not give birth."

　　"那就是說天堂裡的人口是永遠不變的？"

"Does it mean that the population in Heaven always stays the same?"

　　"那也不見得。當一個神仙犯了大的錯誤，他或她便會被罰下人間像人們一樣去接受苦難，如此一來，天堂裡的人口便會少了一個。"

"Not exactly, when one immortal is found of making a big mistake, he or she will be punished in a way by being sent to the human world, suffering as a human. In that case, the population in Heaven will decrease by one."

　　"這種事情時常發生嗎？"

"Does it happen very often?"

　　"有時發生但不常有，這要看每件事情的個別狀況而定。如果只是個小的錯誤，這個神仙便會被剝奪他或她的超

自然的神力及罰去人間一段時光，處罰期滿後，這個神仙便
會被准許回到天堂裡來。」

"It happens but not very often, and it depends on the
individual situation. If it is only a mild mistake, the immortal
will be suspended of his or her supernatural powers and be put
in the human world for a certain period of time. After the
punishment is over, the immortal will be permitted to return to
Heaven again. "

「另一種情況也會偶或發生，」織成繼續說，「當人間
的一個凡人或是幽靈或者動物或者陰間的鬼魂知道如何去依
照天堂裡的定律嚴格去修行的話，這個凡人或是幽靈或者動
物或者鬼魂便會有機會變成一位神仙。如此一來，天堂裡的
人口便會增加了一個。」

"And another situation also happens occasionally,"
Ze-chen continued, "When a person or a spirit or an animal in
the human world or even in the ghost world knows how to
behave himself or herself well enough totally based on the rules
of Heaven, the person or spirit or an animal will have a good
chance to become an immortal. In that case, the population in
Heaven will increase by one."

「當然，這種事情也不是時常發生的，」她迅速又加上
了一句。泰林搖頭感覺這真是太神奇了。

"Of course, this does not happen very often either," she

quickly added. Tai-lin shook his head in continued amazement.

最後，織成招待泰林去了一家舞廳。在那裡，泰林遇到了很多位其他的美麗仙女，她們穿著各種不同的華麗服裝。除了和織成跳舞外，他也和其他幾位仙女跳了舞。

Finally, Ze-chen entertained Tai-lin at a dancing hall. There Tai-lin met many other pretty fairies wearing different fancy clothes. Besides dancing with Ze-chen, he danced with a few other fairies, too.

當他和一位仙女跳舞時，她問他，“怎麼我從來沒有見過你呀？”

While dancing with another fairy, she asked him, "How come I never saw you before?"

因為織成曾經警告過泰林不要洩露他如何來到天堂的秘密，他沒有直接回答這個問題，不過笑了笑說，“我不太十分喜歡跳舞的。”

As Tai-lin was warned by Ze-chen not to reveal the secret of how he came to Heaven, he did not directly answer the question, but said with a smile, "I don't particularly like dancing."

“可是，你的舞跳得很好，”女孩甜蜜而又狡黠地笑著說。

"But you are dancing very well," the girl said with a sweet but sophisticated smile.

接著兩人之間沉默了幾分鐘。
Then there was a silence between them for a few minutes.

"我的名字叫麗麗，" 女孩打破了沉默又說， "你叫什麼名字？"
"My name is Li-li," the girl said, breaking the quiet that had settled upon them. "What's your name?"

就在泰林告訴了他的名字後音樂停了下來，於是泰林把她送回她的座位後又回到織成的身邊。他把他和麗麗的對話告訴了她，織成沒有說什麼，於是他們繼續跳舞。
Soon after Tai-lin told her his name, the music ended, and Tai-lin walked her to her seat before he returned to Ze-chen. He told Ze-chen of his conversation with Li-li. Ze-chen responded with a silent reply and they danced again.

摟著織成的腰，泰林在心中比較著織成和麗麗這兩個仙女：*她們兩位都很美麗，可是她們是一點兒也不相同的；織成的心地很純，可麗麗就比織成要複雜多了。雖然泰林認識織成也還不到兩天，然而他們似乎像是早已認識好一段時間了；換言之，織成很容易相處，而麗麗好像就不太容易了。*
Holding Ze-chen's waist, Tai-lin compared the two fairies,

Ze-chen and Li-li in his mind. *Both are pretty, but they are different from each other. Ze-chen is much more pure-hearted than Li-li while Li-li is much more complicated than Ze-chen.* Although Tai-lin had known Ze-chen for only less than two days, it seemed that they had known each other for a much longer time. In another words, Ze-chen was easy to deal with while Li-li seemed not.

　　他們跳舞了整整一個下午，一直到舞廳關門了。然後，她把他帶回了家，和前天一樣，他們又吃了一頓愉快的晚餐，飯後他們一起看了一會兒電視，然後一起上床。

They danced for the rest of afternoon until the dancing hall closed its door. Then she took him home. Like the day before, they had another pleasant dinner and afterward they watched television for a while before going to bed.

　　他們迅速脫光了衣服。因為泰林此時已經有了性經驗了，他決定這次不再被動。可是當織成輕輕地將他推倒在床上，教導他新的做愛姿態時，他又不得不完全跟隨著她的方式了。泰林和織成瘋狂地享受著一個男子和一個女子所最希望的享受一直到他們達到了情慾的高潮。

And they quickly removed off all of their clothes. As Tai-lin was not naive about sex as he had been before, he decided he would not be inhibited this time. But he still did not know how to react when Ze-chen gently pushed him onto the bed then taught him some new positions for havinf sex he had to follow her methods. Tai-lin and Ze-chen went wild enjoying whatever a man and a woman wished to do until they reached the height of their passion. .

做完了愛後，泰林認真地問織成她是否可能為他生一個小孩。她笑著回答，"我曾經告訴過你，我們仙女們是不生兒育女的。今天夜裡，你就是我的小乖乖，讓我們享受我們自己吧。"

After making love, Tai-lin seriously asked Ze-chen if there was a possibility she would bear a baby for him. She laughed and replied, "As I told you before, we fairies do not give birth to babies. You're my baby tonight. Let's enjoy ourselves."

不久，這兩個愛人又擁抱又親吻在床上滾來滾去了。他們談笑了一個鐘頭後，泰林又有需要她的感覺了，織成立刻迎了上去，雙方都不想等待什麼。他奮勇前進，直到她的心田，她熱情如火；這個時候，他只知道她是他的，她也明瞭他是她的。

Then they hugged and kissed and rolled over on the bed again. They talked and giggled and laughed together for an hour, and Tai-lin had a desire to want her again. Ze-chen readily opened herself to take him right away. Neither of the two wanted to wait. He drove in, deep into the heart of her, and her heat welcomed him. All they knew was that she was his, and he was hers.

　　"啊，織成！"他愉快地呻吟著。

"Oh, Ze-chen!" he groaned with pleasure.

　　"啊，泰林！"她瘋狂地回應。

"Oh, Tai-lin!" she responded wildly.

　　他們儘情歡樂得汗出如漿，於是織成提議他們一同去沖
個澡，對於泰林來說這又是一椿新鮮玩意，他從來沒有和一
個女人在同一個蓮蓬下淋浴。當織成將水調溫了後，她牽著
泰林的手走進了浴室，在蓮蓬下，他們擁抱接吻不停。然後
織成抓起了肥皂來洗擦泰林全身，洗擦好了她又要泰林用肥
皂來洗擦她的全身。

　　When they were sated and perspiring from their exertions,
Ze-chen suggested they shower together, another new
experience for Tai-lin who had never shared a shower with a
woman. Ze-chen made sure the water was warm enough then
she held Tai-lin's hand and they stepped in under the soothing
spray and they kissed and hugged continuously. Soon Ze-chen
grabbed a bar of soap and began wiping it all over Tai-lin's
body then she handed the soap to him so he could cleanse her.

　　完全揩乾了身體後，兩個人回到床上，一絲不掛地躺
著，由於疲倦，很快就入眠了。第二天醒來時，差不多已經

是中午了。

After drying off, they returned to the bed. While still naked, both of them quickly drifted off to sleep, exhausted from their physical efforts. When they finally woke up the next day, it was almost noontime.

「昨天夜裡是我一生中最甜蜜的時光，」泰林愉悅地告訴織成。

"Last night was the sweetest one I have ever had, even imagined," Tai-lin told Ze-chen joyfully.

「我也有此感覺，」織成帶著一個迷人的笑容回答。

"I had the same feeling, too," Ze-chen answered with a bewitching smile.

日子就是這般地一天天過著。在天堂裡，沒有煩惱，沒有勞心也沒有勞力的工作，只有享受，享受人間人們所最夢寐以求的從對方身體上獲得來的享樂。

Their time passed without worries and no work obligations, only enjoyment and the physical pleasure they took in each other's body, the kind of life most people in the human world dreamed of having.

一個星期後，泰林對於這種沒有一點兒需要努力的生活感到煩悶，他也感覺到織成是個典型的仙女，與人間的女孩是完全地不同；可他是個典型的凡夫俗子，與天堂裡的男性仙人也是完全不同的。短時間相處是有趣，不過如果終生如此，他在人間的女友蘋蘋是比織成更爲適合他的。

A week later, Tai-lin finally became bored of such a no-challenge life without work. He also found that Ze-chen was a typical fairy, totally different from any girl in the human world. But he was a typical mortal, totally different from the male immortal in Heaven, too. For a short period of time, being with each other was fun. But for a lifelong commitment, Pin-pin, his human lover, would be much more suitable for him than Ze-chen.

他把這個想法告訴了織成。她輕聲地回答，"我也有此同感，你是個道地的凡夫俗子，這裡不是你的天下。此外，我還有一點兒擔心你的混入天堂怕被發現。還記得那個曾經和你跳過舞的麗麗嗎？她是個心胸很狹小的女子。假如我把你留在天堂裡太久了，我很害怕她就會去天堂的政府裡要求調查這件事情的。

He expressed his thought to Ze-chen. She replied softly, "I understand as I have the same feeling, too. You are absolutely a mortal. This is not your world. Besides, I'm a little worried about the discovery of your sneaking into Heaven. Remember Li-li, the girl you danced with her in the dancing hall the other day? She is a very narrow-minded woman. If I keep you with me for too long, I'm afraid she may report me to the Heaven government and ask for an investigation."

然後，她嘆了口氣又接著說，"很可能我們的情侶關係必須告一段落了。"

Then she sighed and added, "Maybe our relationship as lovers is coming to an end."

就像她上次如何把他帶到天堂一樣，第二天早上她把他又帶回到了地面上。

Like the way she had taken him to Heaven, she took him back to the earth the next morning.

第四章　Chapter Four

因為泰林在天堂的購貨中心裡曾經拿了一小袋子的鑽石首飾，他想當他在人間將這些鑽石首飾賣出後，他一定會發筆大財的。但是，在他到達地面想把小袋子從口袋裡掏出時，他驚訝地發現小袋子沒有了。他記得很清楚，在織成送他回到人間前，他還特別檢查過他的口袋一次。

As Tai-lin had collected a small bag of diamond jewelry from a chopping center in Heaven, he thought he would have good fortune in the human world after selling those diamonds. But soon after reaching ground, he tried to take out the bag from his pocket and was surprised to find that the bag was not there. He remembered clearly he had checked his pocket before

Ze-chen took him back to the earth.

　　*莫非是在返回人間的途中遺失了的？是神秘的天堂發現了後把它收回去了嗎？如果真是的，他們是如何做到的？織成知道這件事情嗎？也許就是她用她的超自然法力拿回去了的？*他無法去證實他的任何一種猜測，而且也無人可問。突然間，他懷疑他是否真的去過了天堂，也許這不過只是一個荒謬的怪夢。

　　Could it have been lost on the way of returning to the human world? Or could it have been discovered and taken away by the mysterious world of Heaven? If so, how could they do it? Did Ze-chen know about it? Maybe it was she who used her supernatural power to take it back? But he could not confirm any of his assumptions and had no one to ask. Suddenly, he wondered if he had actually gone to Heaven, or if he just had experienced a fabulous and exciting but eerie dream.

　　當他返回康復成衣工廠工作時，他被告知因爲他沒有於事前獲得准許而竟離職一個多禮拜，他已經被開除了。明顯地，他去天堂一事是千真萬確的。

　　When he returned to his job at Comfort Garment Factory, he was told that because he had been absent for more than a week without advance permission, he was fired. Obviously, then he understood that his experiences in Heaven had been real.

他乃急忙去見他的副總經理舅父，解釋他在峨眉山上跌了一跤，傷得很重差點喪失了性命，幸得一個住在山腳下的農夫搭救了他，好心的農夫把他帶回了家去。因為山區沒有電話或郵局，他無法向他的上級報告。

He hurriedly went to see his uncle, the assistant general manager, explaining that he had a fall on E-Mei Mountain and had been injured badly and almost died. Luckily, he was discovered and rescued by a farmer who lived by the foot of mountain. The kind farmer took him home. As there was no telephone or post office in the mountain area, he simply had no way to notify his boss in the factory.

由於他的有力親戚幫助，同時也因為他過去的工作業績實在優異，結果泰林的工作又保住了。他和蘋蘋也和好如初。時間就這樣一天天地過去，好像什麼事情也沒有發生。他知道如果他告訴別人他曾經去過了天堂，是沒有一個人會相信他的話的，因此索性一句話也不說就連對蘋蘋也不講。

With the help of his powerful relative and also partly because of his excellent working record, Tai-lin was reinstated in his job. He and Pin-pin went back as lovers again. Things went on as if nothing had happened. Realizing that he wouldn't be believed about his trip to Heaven, he remained silent and told no one of his adventure, not even Pin-pin.

這時學習英文已經漸漸地成為全國的風尚，成衣工廠總經理向當地一家專科學校聘請了一位教師來工廠裡為他的員工們補習英文。對於蘋蘋來說，這真是一個天大的好消息，她把那鎮上的英文班停了，因為那個班級她要付錢的，參加了工廠裡的英文班，因為這對員工是免費的。

Because English was becoming more popular in the nation now, the general manager of the garment factory hired a teacher from a nearby college to tutor his employees English. It was indeed happy news for Pin-pin. She dropped her English class in town, for which she had to pay, and joined the factory English class, which was free for the employees.

同時她也鼓勵泰林參加這個免費英文班，當泰林還在猶豫時，他的副總經理舅父也希望泰林不要失掉這個大好良機，因為他自己也參加這個英文班了。終於，泰林沒有選擇，只好和蘋蘋一起進入英文班就讀。

Meanwhile, she encouraged Tai-lin to attend the free English lessons as well. While Tai-lin still hesitated, his uncle, the assistant general manager, also urged Tai-lin to take advantage of the chance as he himself attended the class, too. Finally, Tai-lin had no choice but to join Pin-pin in the English class.

泰林一旦投入，除了工作外，幾乎不停地每天早晚都在勤讀英文，因而進步得很快。因為有了進步，他讀起來也就更有勁了。這使得蘋蘋非常高興。

Once he started, Tai-lin made rapid progress. He spent all his spare time, morning and evening, studying English as hard as he could. Because of having progress, he studied more diligently. His devotion made Pin-pin very happy.

也許有一天泰林會和我一起去美國。如果真的那樣，那該有多好，她想。

Maybe one of these days, Tai-lin will go to the United States with me. How wonderful it would be if that could really happen, she thought.

可是，事情發生出乎她的意料之外。

But things went on beyond what she wished for.

那個蘋蘋的朋友的朋友，曾經去過美國還在那兒停留了兩年半光景回來後帶回了兩萬美元的女子，一天來拜訪蘋蘋，告訴她一個好消息。

The girl, Pin-pin's friend's friend, who had been in the United States for two and a half years and brought back twenty thousand dollars in US currency, visited Pin-pin one day telling her good news.

根據這個女子，她上次去美國是透過一個秘密管道，嚴格說是個非法途徑，她付與一個神秘的中間人三萬兩千元人民幣幫她偷渡到了美國。她沒有這筆錢，她向她的有錢姑母借的。

According to the girl, she had gone through a secret channel, an illegal way technically speaking, to set to the United States last time by paying a mysterious middleman thirty-two thousand yuans to help her sneak into America. Since she did not have the money, she borrowed it from her wealthy aunt.

在美國，她在紐約中國飯店裡工作賺了大錢。不過一年光景，她就把她的債務還清了。當她回到中國的時候，她已經儲蓄了兩萬多美元。這個女子說她計劃再幹一次，她問蘋蘋這次要不要與她一起去。

In America, she worked for the Chinese restaurants in New York earning good money. In a year, she paid off her debt. By the time she returned to China, she had saved up more than twenty thousand dollars of American currency. The girl said that she planned to do it once again, asking Pin-pin if she wanted to join her this time.

"你到了美國後，沒有人會問你如何來到這個國家的。你就可以大賺美國錢，儘情地去享受，"這個女子興奮地告訴蘋蘋。

"After you enter America, nobody will ask you how you came to this country. You can then make the damn good American money and enjoy whatever you want," the girl told

Pin-pin excitedly.

在蘋蘋還沒有回答時，她又問她，"你要和我一起去嗎？"

Before Pin-pin answered, the girl asked her again, "Do you want to go with me?"

"當然，我要去的，"蘋蘋不加思索地回答。

"Of course, I want to go," Pin-pin replied without hesitation.

可是當她再一考慮後，蘋蘋對這個女子說，"但是，我沒有這麼多錢去付中間人。"

After a second thought, Pin-pin said to the woman, "But I don't have so much of money to pay the middleman."

"你可以向你有錢的親戚借啊，就像我第一次的一樣。"

"You can borrow it from your rich relatives as I did the first time."

"可是我沒有任何有錢的親戚。"

"But, I don't have any rich relatives."

"你為什麼不向你的男朋友泰林去借？每個人都知道他已經存了一大筆錢。"

"Why don't you ask your boyfriend Tai-lin to lend it to you? Everybody knows that he has saved up a lot of money."

"是的，他是有錢。"突然間，蘋蘋又興奮了起來。
"Yes, he has." Suddenly, Pin-pin became excited again.

在我到達美國開始賺大錢後，我一定會盡全力把泰林也弄到新大陸和我在一塊，然後我們在那兒結婚，和美國人民同樣地享受豪華的生活。

After I reach America and start to make the damn good money, I'll try every way I can to make Tai-lin join me in the new land. Then we'll marry there and enjoy the most luxurious life like American people do.

她愈想就愈興奮。
The more she thought about it, the more excited she became.

散工後，她邀請泰林到一家小飯店吃飯。那兒她愉快地告訴他她的計劃。
Soon after work, she invited Tai-lin to eat at a small restaurant where she joyfully told him her plan.

聽了她的故事後，泰林以堅定嚴肅的語氣說，"是的，我是儲蓄了三萬塊錢，那是我準備用在我們結婚上的。現在，你要把它用在我從來不同意的途徑上，對不起，我不能讓你去做。這在中國和美國都是違法的，當你被抓到時，你便會什麼都沒有了只有大的麻煩。我是完全絕對不同意這個冒險方案的。"

After listening to her story, Tai-lin said obstinately and seriously, "Yes, I do have the thirty thousand yuans. I have saved it up for our marriage. Now you want to use it in a way I never agreed to. Sorry, I cannot let you do it. It's illegal in both China and United States. When you are caught, you will have nothing but big trouble. I simply can not agree to this adventure at all."

斷然的拒絕使得蘋蘋大怒。她迅速地站了起來，尖銳地向著泰林吼道，"聽著，蔡泰林！我們的關係是到此為止了，你不再是我的朋友了！"接著她衝出了飯店，連那已經放在桌子上的飯菜都不吃了。

His outright refusal made Pin-pin furious. She quickly stood up and sharply yelled at Tai-lin, "Listen, Tai-lin Cai, our relationship has come to an end! You're not my friend anymore!" Then she rushed out of the restaurant without even eating the meal which had already been served on the table.

真的從第二天開始，不管泰林如何想法去接近她，她就是不再和他講話了。

Indeed, from the next day on, she would not speak to

Tai-lin again, no matter how hard he tried to approach her.

當她和別的同事們有說有笑時，只要見到泰林走過，就立刻走開了，她把泰林當作一個陌生人看待。

When she and other colleagues were talking and laughing, as soon as she saw Tai-lin heading toward her, she would immediately walk away. She treated him as a stranger.

泰林感到難過極了，可他沒有辦法使蘋蘋改變她的想法。他懷念那個仙女織成，她永遠是那麼地快樂，從不煩惱什麼，也從不向任何人發脾氣。也許因為她是仙女，蘋蘋不過是一個平凡的人間女子。因為他自己也是一個平凡的人間男子，他瞭解他是不可能與一個仙女永遠在一起的，他必須和人間的平凡女子在一起。可是，這個人間的平凡女子是這麼地難以對付！他不停地去想如何改善他與蘋蘋的關係，可就是無法找出一條路來。

Tai-lin was hurt deeply, but he had no idea of how he could get Pin-pin to change her mind. He missed the fairy, Ze-chen. She was happy all the time, never worried about anything, nor became angry at anyone. Maybe it was because she was a fairy, and Pin-pin was an ordinary female mortal. As an ordinary male mortal, he realized that he could not be with a fairy in Heaven forever. He must be with an ordinary female mortal, but this particular ordinary female mortal was so difficult to get along with. He kept thinking about how to improve his relationship with Pin-pin, but he could not find a way out.

　　而他的痛苦是與日俱增。他開始每天晚間去飲烈酒，希望酒精能夠幫助他解決煩惱，至少可以麻醉他的感受及對蘋蘋的懷念。然而他酒飲得愈多，煩惱也就愈多。

And the headache began to bother him daily. He started to drink hard liquor every evening in hopes that the alcohol could help him solve his problems or at least numb his feelings and his longing for Pin-pin. But the more liquor he drank, the more problems he encountered.

　　終於，在一個晚間，當他獨自一個人在他的公寓裡飲了一整瓶的茅臺（一種最強烈的中國威士卡）後，他喝醉了，特別感到自悲，他將一根繩子綁在天花板的燈柱上，另一端套在他的頸子上，爬上了一隻高椅子，揩乾了眼淚，泰林把他腳下的椅子一腳蹬開。

Finally, after drinking a whole bottle of Mao Tai - one of the hardest Chinese whiskeys - alone one night in his apartment, he became drunk and filled with self pity. He tied a rope around a ceiling light fixture, looped the other end around his neck, climbed on top of a chair. After wiping tears from eyes, Tai-lin kicked the chair out from beneath him.

　　兩天後，他的舅父關心泰林怎麼又不上班了，他來公寓一看，傷心地發現泰林早已死亡了。

Two days later, when he was finally discovered by his uncle, who was concerned that Tai-lin had missed his work again, he came to the apartment and sadly found Tai-lin was dead already.

第五章　Chapter Five

泰林死後變成了鬼。他知道他已經離開了人世，現在是在陰間了。他獨自在一條荒涼的路上走著，不知道要到何處去。不久，他走到了一個小集鎮，發現了很多的人，不，不是人，是很多的鬼，和人間的任何一個集鎮上的人們一樣在忙忙碌碌地做買賣，他認為這兩個世界簡直沒有什麼不同。

After death, Tai-lin became a ghost. He realized that he had left the human world and entered the ghost world. He walked on a lonely road, wondering where he should go. Soon, he reached a small town and found many people, no, not people, many ghosts, doing business as industriously as workers in any city in the world of humans. He could not readily find any difference between the two worlds.

當他在街道上逛蕩時，他偶然從遠處看到了一個男子，看起來好像是蠻熟習的，於是他向這個男子走去。突然間，這個男子與泰林都驚訝了。這是顧成，泰林的一個好朋友。

While he was wandering thought the streets, he happened

to see a man in a distance who looked somewhat familiar to him, so he approached the man. Suddenly, both the man and Tai-lin were surprised. That was Gu Cheng, a good friend of Tai-lin.

顧成與泰林是中學同班同學，而且兩人又是好朋友。顧成於兩年前死於一場車禍。作爲一個好朋友，泰林不但迅速去看望顧成的寡母安慰她並參加了他的葬禮，更經常去拜訪這位老婦人並儘可能地給與幫助，一直到她於一年後也亡故了。顧成很感激泰林在陽間照顧他的母親，可沒有辦法向他說聲道謝。

Gu Cheng and Tai-lin were classmates in high school, and they were good friends. Sadly Gu Cheng had died of an automobile crash a couple of years earlier. Being a good friend, Tai-lin not only paid a quick visit to Gu Cheng's widowed mother to comfort her and attended his funeral, but also often went to see the old lady and gave her helps as much as he could until she died a year later. Gu Cheng was grateful for Tai-lin's caring for his mother in the human world but had no way to say thanks to him.

現在他們在陰間不期而遇了。顧成邀請泰林回家，並訊問他的死因。

Now they unexpectedly met in the world of ghosts. Gu Cheng invited Tai-lin to his home and inquired about the cause of his death.

　　瞭解了泰林的故事後，顧成要泰林暫時就住在他的家裡，直到他有了工作及他自己的家。

After hearing Tai-lin's story, Gu Cheng offered to let Tai-lin stay at his home temporarily until he found a job and a home for himself.

顧成告訴泰林，如果一個人死於自然死亡包括意外災難，陰間的最高統治者閻羅王就會派一士兵去把這個人的靈魂帶來他的辦公室。在辦公室登記完了以後，這個鬼魂便會被釋放，可以自由地去做他或她想要做的任何事情。但是，當閻羅王辦公室安排這個鬼的投胎時間到了時，一般說來是變成鬼三年後，這個鬼必須向閻羅王辦公室報到，沒有選擇地接受安排投胎。這是陰間的法律，每一個鬼必須服從。

Gu Cheng told Tai-lin that if a person died of a natural death, including accidents, the grand ruler of the ghost world, Hades, would send a solider to take the person's spirit to his office. After registered with the office, the ghost would be released and be free to do whatever he or she wanted. But when the time of rebirth for the ghost arranged by the Hades' office came, usually three years after a person's death, the ghost had to report to the Hades' office to take the arrangement without any choice. It was the law in the ghost world. Every ghost must obey.

　　事實上，所有的鬼都企盼早日投胎爲人。至於投胎到那

一類的人家，及將來他或她又會變成個什麼樣的人，這完全
憑藉著這個鬼生前為人時的所作所為。如果這個人曾經做過
很多的善事，非常可能這個鬼便會被投生在一個富裕的人
家，或成為一個成功的人，享受舒適的人生。如果這個人曾
經做過很多的惡事，這個鬼便會被處罰生在一個非常貧窮的
人家，或是成為一個不幸的人，一生遭受著無盡的苦痛。

In fact, all the ghosts expected to be reborn as human
beings again. As for which kind of family to be born to or what
kind of person he or she would become, it totally depended
upon the deeds the ghost had performed while he or she was a
human. If the person had performed many good deeds, most
likely the ghost would be born to a wealthy family or become a
successful person who would enjoy a good life. If the person
had committed many evils, the ghost would be punished by
being born to a very poor family or becoming an unfortunate
person, suffering all kinds of misfortune.

至於那些自殺的人們，因為在閻羅王的辦公室裡是沒有
這些鬼的記錄的，這些鬼必須自動向陰間政府報到，並請求
當投胎時間到了後也安排投胎，否則，這些鬼魂將永遠是陰
間的鬼魂了。

For the people who died of committing suicide, there were
no records for those ghosts in the Hades' office. Those ghosts
must voluntarily report to the government office and beg for
arrangements of rebirth when the time came. If not, they would

become ghosts forever in the ghost world.

　　第二天，顧成幫助泰林到閻羅王的辦公室辦理了報到的手續，閻羅王的助手們也答應泰林三年後將安排他的重生。然後，泰林就必須安排他在陰間等待投胎的生活了。

　　The next day, Gu Cheng helped Tai-lin make report at the Hades' office, and the Hades' assistants promised Tai-lin to arrange a rebirth for him three years later. After that, Tai-lin must arrange his life in the world of ghosts while waiting for his rebirth.

　　顧成是一家大百貨公司裡的總經理，因為泰林熟悉成衣，他僱用泰林在他的成衣部門作為一個售貨員。在收到第一個月的薪金後，泰林搬出了顧成的家，租了一棟小公寓，獨立生活了。

　　Since Gu Cheng was managing a big department store, he hired Tai-lin to work in his clothing department as a salesman because Tai-lin was familiar with those products. After receiving his first month's salary, Tai-lin moved out of Gu Cheng's home and rented a small apartment to become independent.

　　一個半月後，銷售部又僱了一名女銷售員。那是一個秀麗的年輕女孩名叫馨蒂。馨蒂在陽間出生於一個富裕的家庭，可是她不喜歡去學校讀書，在她還是十五歲時就從初中裡退學了，經常和一些不良青少年們鬼混。終於，她離家出走了，加入了一個幫派，從事各種非法活動。當她在與夥伴們搶劫銀行時，於槍戰中被擊中，送到醫院急診室時就死亡了。

One and half months later, a teenage girl was hired in the sales department as a saleswoman. She was an attractive young woman named Xin-di. In the human world, Xin-di was from a wealthy family, but she did not like to go to school. She dropped out of junior high school when she was fifteen, and spent her time hanging out with juvenile delinquents all the time. Finally she ran away from home and joined a gang, committing all kinds of illegal activities. Once when she and a few others were robbing a bank, she was shot during a fight. Soon after, she died in the hospital emergency room.

雖然現在已經是個鬼了，她可仍然是無憂無慮的，什麼也不憂愁，是個典型的樂天派年輕女子。她告訴泰林她三年後投胎為人後，她一定要做個好女孩絕對不再做壞事了，她明瞭她可能不會再生在富裕的人家，因此，她必須要加倍努力才能在來生做個成功的人。

Even though she was a ghost now, she was still carefree, worrying about nothing, a typical happy-go-lucky type of young woman. She told Tai-lin that three years later after being reborn as a person, she would try to be a nice girl and would not do any bad deeds. She realized that she probably would not be born to a wealthy family again, so she must struggle hard for her future in order to become successful in her next life.

　　因為她對成衣不太在行，尤其是男子及小孩的衣服更不瞭解，因而在工作上泰林不時給予她幫助，他們兩個很快地便建立了友誼。由於日日的接觸，一個月後泰林和馨蒂就墜入了愛河。為了節省公寓的房租，他和她乃索性搬住在一起。對於其他的鬼友們來說，他們不過是合夥租房者，實際上，他們生活在一起就像一對恩愛的夫妻，雖然他們並沒有真正的結婚。

As she knew almost nothing about the garments particularly the ones for men and children, Tai-lin helped her and they soon established a good friendship. With daily contact a month later, Tai-lin and Xin-di fell in love. In order to save rent, he and she agreed to live together. In the eyes of others, they were only roommates, but in actually they lived as beloved husband and wife although they were not legally married.

　　"泰林，"一天晚間，當他們吃完晚飯後閑談時，馨蒂問他，"你已經在陰間有好一段時間了。與陽間的生活相比，你認為陰間如何？"

"Tai-lin," Xin-di asked him one evening while they were chatting after supper, "you have been in the ghost world for a while. How do you think the life here compare to that in the human world?"

　　"我告訴過你，我還曾經去過天堂呢。在這三個世界裡，坦白說來，我還是喜歡做為一個人，居住在人的世界裡。"

"As I told you before, I have also been in Heaven. Among the three worlds, honestly speaking, I still love being a human, living in the world of human beings."

　　"我不同意你的意見，"馨蒂說。"天堂是如此地美好，如果我能有機會成為一個仙女，我將永遠居住在天堂裡。"

"I don't agree with you," Xin-di said. "Heaven sounds so wonderful. If I could have a chance to become a fairy, I would try to stay in Heaven forever."

　　"那的確是每個人都如此想的，"泰林說。"但是，如果你在那裡居住了一陣子以後，你的感覺就會不一樣了。舉例來說，每一個鬼都希望能夠投生在一個富裕的人家。但是，據我所瞭解，並不是陽間所有富裕的人們一天到晚都是快樂的。根據統計，富裕人們自殺的比例比貧窮人家還要多些。這個意思就是說生活在奢侈中的人並不保證會有一個美滿的人生。這就像那居住在美國外的人們往往會錯誤地認為住在美國的人們都會比他們快樂。"

"Well, that's what everybody thinks," Tai-lin said. "But once you are there for a while, you will feel differently. For instance, every ghost wishes to be reborn to a wealthy family, but, as I understand it not all wealthy people in the world of humans are happy all the time. Statistics indicate that the suicide rate of the wealthy is higher than that of poor people. It means that living in luxury does not guarantee a happy life. It is just like that the people living outside of the United States always mistakenly thinking the people in the United States are happier than them."

"但是，你的陽間愛人蘋蘋在這一點上就從來沒有同意過你，對吧？"馨蒂喜歡惡作劇，她故意刺痛泰林的最痛處。

"But your human lover, Pin-pin, never agreed with you on this subject, right?" Xin-di liked to play tricks and she purposely touched Tai-lin's most painful issue.

"那就是我為什麼要自殺，"泰林怒氣衝沖地回答。

"That's exactly the reason why I committed suicide," Tai-lin replied angrily.

"抱歉，我不應該向你提及這事，"馨蒂急忙地道歉。

"Sorry, I should not have mentioned this to you," Xin-di quickly apologized.

"沒有關係，"泰林說。"我已經把過去的一切都忘記了。"

"That's all right," Tai-lin said. "I have forgotten all of the past."

雖然泰林說他已經把他在陽間的過去都忘記了，事實上，他從來沒有。而且一經提及，他就無法阻止他的回憶過去像泉水一樣地不停流出。

Although Tai-lin said that he had forgotten his past in the human world, in fact, he never did. Once it was mentioned, he just could not stop his memories streaming back like the constant flow from a spring.

不知道蘋蘋現在怎麼樣了？ 她是否仍是夢想去美國？抑或她已經去了那裡？如果她已經去了，她在那新大陸快樂嗎？泰林不停地想著這些問題，他把他的秘密隱藏在他的內心深處，不讓馨蒂知道。

How is Pin-pin doing now? Is she still dreaming of going to the United States, or has she already been there? If she has, is she happy in the new land? Tai-lin kept thinking of those questions, but he hid his secrets deep in his heart and would not let Xin-di know it.

慢慢地，泰林發現在陰間，閻羅王管理眾鬼並不像陽間一些統治者那樣地嚴格。當某一個鬼投胎為人的時間到了，這個鬼將被通知到閻羅王的辦公處接受安排。除此外，眾鬼們可以隨意去做他們要做的事情。

Gradually, Tai-lin found that in the world of ghosts, Hades did not rule the ghosts as strictly as some of the rulers in the human world. When it was time for a certain ghost to be reborn as a human, the ghost would be notified and go to the Hades' office to take the arrangement. Other than that, the ghosts could do anything they wanted.

因為每一個鬼在向陰間政府報到三年後就會有一個投胎為人的機會，所以所有的鬼都不像人間的人們那樣地努力工作。他們工作不過是為生活費用或是消磨時間而已，沒有一個鬼有什麼野心或長期計劃的。馨蒂就是其中的這麼一個。

Because every ghost would be given a chance to be reborn as a person three years after he or she reported to the ghost government, there was no incentive for them to work as hard as people did in the human world. Ghosts worked simply to earn a living or to kill time. No ghost had any big ambitions or long-term plans. Xin-di was one of them.

馨蒂沒有什麼計劃，不過享受她所能享受的，她與蘋蘋不同。蘋蘋一心一意夢想去美國，去賺更多的錢，和其他很多的人們一樣，去買豪華的東西，希望永遠享有。馨蒂一天到晚都是快樂的，她沒有野心，對當前總是滿意的，享受她所享受的，她是一個很好相處的鬼。

Xin-di had no plans for her future but enjoyed whatever she could. In that regard she was different from Pin-pin. Pin-pin dreamed of going to the United States to make more money, to buy luxurious things like most of the other people who wanted to own all the good things forever and forever. Xin-di was happy all the time. Content with what she was, and enjoyed what she had, she was easy to deal with.

終於，泰林對他目前的生活感到無比的厭倦，可是他無法選擇他自己的生活方式。他到陰間已經半年了，還有那兩年半的日子在等待著他才可以讓政府為他安排投胎重新為人。兩年半的日子對他來說是多麼地漫長。突然，他為他的自殺感到非常後悔。

Finally, Tai-lin became very bored of this kind of life, yet he could not choose his own way of life. He had been in the ghost world for half a year, and still had another two and a half years before an official arrangement would be made for his rebirth. Two and a half years seemed like an eternity to him. Suddenly, he very much regretted his committing suicide.

假如他能夠早知道陰間是這麼樣子的話，他是絕對不會自己了斷他在人生間的生命的。他記得一句中國老話說：好死不如惡活。

If he could have known what the world of ghosts was truly like, he definitely would not have ended his life in the human world. He remembered an old Chinese saying: No matter how terrible a human's life was, it would still be better than a good life in the ghost world.

但是一切都是太晚了。他已經不是一個人而是個鬼了。

他把他的想法告訴馨蒂，可是她不同意他，她說他們都早已離開陽世了，再多的後悔也與事無補的。她很有耐心在等待投胎的時間到來。所以，她儘可能地使她過得舒服而什麼也不去憂愁。

But it was too late. He was no longer a person but a ghost. He told Xin-di what he thought. She did not agree with him. She said since they had already left the human world, no matter how much regret they had, it would not help. She was very patient in waiting for the time to be reborn. Therefore, she tried to live as comfortably as she could and worried about nothing.

雖然泰林不同意馨蒂，可他也沒有其他的方法去安排他的生活。突然間，他有一個奇怪的想法，他想溜回陽間去看看一切是否仍和過去一樣。這就好像一個離開家鄉很久的遊子，仍然不時關懷他出生及曾經住過多年的地方，所以泰林非常懷念陽世。

Although Tai-lin did not agree with Xin-di, he had no other way to arrange his life. Suddenly, he had a strange idea. He planned to sneak back to the world of humans to see if everything was still the same. It was like when a person had left his hometown for some time, he would often miss the place he was born and had lived for many years. So Tai-lin was missing the world of human beings very much.

他終於說服了馨蒂讓他回去陽間三天。馨蒂明瞭他仍在懷念他的陽間愛人蘋蘋。因爲她和他畢竟沒有正式結婚，她知道讓他回去陽間匆忙一遊可能使他將來不再懷念陽間了，便會有耐心地和她在陰間一起等待那最後的兩年半時間而不再有什麼埋怨。於是她答應他她會代他向他們的上級爲他請求三天的病假。泰林也答允馨蒂他在第四天時一定會回來的。

He finally convinced Xin-di to let him go back to the human world for three days. Xin-di realized that he still yearned for his human lover, Pin-pin. Since she and he were not legally married, she knew that letting him go back for a quick visit would probably eliminate his desire for the human world allowing him to patiently spend the last two and half years with her in the ghost world without more complaints. So she promised him she would ask their boss, on his behalf, to let him have sick leave for three days. Tai-lin also promised her that he would definitely come back on the fourth day.

　　然後，他便離開了他和馨蒂居住的公寓不聲不響地向陽世走去。

Without fanfare, he left the apartment where he and Xin-di lived and began his journey back to the human world.

第六章　Chapter Six

　　泰林回到了陽間，可他不能像人一樣地出現，因爲鬼只能在晚間出沒。他看見人，可人是看不見他的。他聽到人講話，可人聽不到他說話。

So Tai-lin was back in the world of humans, but he could not appear as a human did. As a ghost, he could only appear in the evening. He saw people, but people could not see him. He heard people speak, but people could not hear him.

如同馨蒂所猜測的，他回到人間後的第一件事便是去拜訪他以前的情人，蘋蘋。

As Xin-di suspected, the first thing he planned to do after returning to the human world was to pay a visit to his former lover, Pin-pin.

天黑了以後，他到蘋蘋那裡去，發現她正在讀一本英文書。很明顯地，她沒有去美國，可能因為她沒有湊到三萬兩千元付中間人。假如他當初借錢給她，她將早已走了。假如他將錢借給她，他也不會去自殺。現在，他死了，可他也沒有把他的錢帶去陰間。突然間，他感到很後悔，同時也明瞭他真是一個傻瓜。這就好像世界上有很多吝嗇的人，他們在世時捨不得花費他們賺來的一文錢，可是死亡後，他們仍把他們的財富留在人世間。

After dark, he went to Pin-pin's home and saw her studying a book in English. Obviously, she had not gone to America, probably because she did not collect the necessary thirty-two thousand yuans to pay the middleman. If he had lent her the money, she would have already gone. And if he had done so, he would not have committed suicide. Now he was dead, and he could not take his money with him to the world of ghosts. Suddenly, he felt very sorry and realized that what he had done was indeed very stupid. It was like that many miserly people did not want to spend one penny but saved all the money they had made. But after death, they still left all their fortune behind in the human world.

人們真是這麼一種奇怪而又愚笨的東西！
People are indeed such strange and stupid creatures!

凝望中，泰林發現雖然沒有他在她的身邊，蘋蘋仍然快樂地在做她想做的事情，而且也沒有懷念他的意思。也許她在發現他死亡時曾經難過過，可誰又知道呢？現在，她看起來像很愉快的。

While watching, Tai-lin found that without him by her side, Pin-pin was still happy and did not show a way of missing him. Maybe she did and had been very sad soon after he died. Who knew? But now, she appeared to be happy.

當他繼續凝望時，他發現她向著牆上的鐘望去，時間是下午六時三十分，她把書放下，拿起了一份請帖上面印著很大的中國字：慶祝建廠十週年茶會。泰林記得這個日子，當他還在陽世時，每年此日，他都會和蘋蘋一起去參加這個慶祝會的。今年，蘋蘋可能要一個人去參加了。

While he kept watching, he noticed that she took a look at the clock on the wall. It was six thirty in the evening. Then she put her book down and picked up a printed invitation with big Chinese characters on it: <u>Celebration Tea Party for Tenth Anniversary of Establishing Factory</u>. Tai-lin remembered that date. While he was a human, he and Pin-pin attended the celebration party together every year. This year, Pin-pin would probably attend the party by herself.

　　放下了請帖，她去她的衣櫥裡去選一件衣服穿去參加茶會。她取出了一件鑲著金邊的粉紅色毛衣，在衣服的左上方繡著一朵紅色的花朵，這是他在她二十歲生日時送給她的生日禮品。因為品質和式樣都很別致，蘋蘋非常喜歡，除了像今天這一類的重大節日外，她在平時是捨不得穿它的。

Putting down the invitation, she went to her closet to choose a dress to wear for the party. She took out a pink sweater with a gold border pattern and a big silk embroidered red flower on the upper left. It was a gift sent to her by him on her twentieth birthday. As both the material and the design were unique, Pin-pin loved it very much and she did not want to wear it on normal days but only on some big occasions like today's party.

　　泰林很有興趣地繼續凝望著。他不久發現蘋蘋把毛衣甩到床上，而她自己也扒到床上大聲痛哭了起來。她悲傷地哭著，並大聲叫著泰林的名字。她不停地責備自己說是她殺害了泰林。「如果我不向她借錢，他是不會自殺的。這是我一生中最大的遺憾，我殺了他！我欠他的太多了！可是，我沒有辦法去償還他了。」

Tai-lin was happy to keep watching, but he soon noticed that Pin-pin suddenly threw the sweater on her bed and then climbed on the bed, and began crying loudly. She was crying bitterly and calling Tai-lin's name. She kept blaming herself that it was she who killed Tai-lin. "If I had not asked him to lend me money, he would not have killed himself. It was my biggest regret in my life. I killed him! I owe him too much! And I have no way to repay him."

在巨大的悲痛中，她宣佈，「啊，老天爺呀，如果您能讓泰林復活，我將接受他的求婚，不管他要去美國與否都立刻嫁給他。」

While crying in great sorrow, she declared, "Oh, Heaven, if You could have Tai-lin revived, I would accept his courting and marry him right away no matter whether he wants to go to America or not."

在聽了這麼一個宣佈後，泰林震撼極了。他立刻跑了過去想擁抱蘋蘋而完全忘記了他現在不是一個人而是個鬼了。鬼是不能接觸到人的身體的，就好像是一陣風吹過人是毫無感覺的。突然裡，泰林感到一生中最大的悔歉。他發誓一定要儘全力去設法復活爲一個人，和他的甜蜜的愛人蘋蘋結婚。

Hearing such a declaration, Tai-lin was stunned. He immediately rushed over trying to hug Pin-pin, forgetting that he now was not a human but a ghost. A ghost could not touch a human's body, like a blowing wind totally unfelt by the person. All of a sudden, Tai-lin felt the greatest regret he had ever had. He swore he must try all he could to be revived as a human again and marry his sweetheart, the lovely Pin-pin.

於是，他想起了多年前他曾經讀過一些描寫靈異的書籍，其中說道一個鬼可以用借屍還魂的方法重新復活過來，這個復活過來的人看起來和他未死前一模一樣，不過靈魂則是這個鬼的靈魂。

Then he remembered that he had read some mysterious books years ago saying that a ghost could be revived as a human by a way of borrowing another newly dead person's body. It meant that the revived person would appear as the one before death, but the soul would be that of the ghost's.

這是一個多麼興奮的主意。泰林大喜過望。他不想再去凝望蘋蘋的哭泣了，他要儘快復活和蘋蘋在一起，必要的時候還去安慰她。

It was an exciting idea. Tai-lin was elated. He did not want to keep watching Pin-pin's crying. He wanted to be revived as soon as possible, so he could be reunited with her and comfort her when needed.

　　他溜出了蘋蘋的房間，跑到街道上去尋找一個剛死的人，從一條街走到另一條街沒有一個確切的目的地。經過了一整夜的搜索，他毫無所獲。第二個夜晚，他也沒有找到一個死人。

He sneaked out of Pin-pin's home and onto the streets to look for a newly dead human. He traveled around from one street to another without a definite destination. After a whole night's searching, he did not find a single dead human. And the second night was as equally unsuccessful.

　　他明瞭假如他在第三個晚上仍然達不成他的願望，他必須回到鬼的世界恢復他的舊日生活，和馨蒂在一起度過那最後的兩年半日子才可以重生為一個人。

He realized that if he could not fulfill his wish to be revived the third night, he must return to the world of ghosts and resume his old way of life with Xin-di for the remaining two and half years before his rebirth as a human.

　　當黑暗籠罩著大地後的第三個夜晚，他溜進了一家醫院。他在想既然這裡是為病人而設的地方，一些病人總會死的。他發現很多位病得很重的的病人，可沒有一個病人看起來像要死的。然後，他來到了急診室，看到了好幾個病人的病情都很危急，可也沒有一個人像很快就要死亡的樣子。他很失望，準備離開這家醫院到另一家去。

When the darkness descended over the land in the third night, he sneaked into a hospital. He thought since this was a place for patients, some patients would die. He found many patients, and some were extremely ill, but none of them seemed to be dying. Then he came to the emergency room and saw several patients in critical conditions but still none looked as if death was imminent. He was disappointed and planned to leave this hospital for another one.

就在他離開前，他突然聽到了一個像醫生樣子的中年男子告訴一個年輕的女護士，四號病房裡的男病人已經死亡了，他要她馬上通知死者的家屬。

Before he was out of the door, he heard a middle-aged man like a doctor tell a young female nurse that the male patient in Unit Four had passed away. He asked her to notify the dead man's family right away.

一個男子已經死亡了！
A man has passed away!

泰林大喜過望，立刻一頭奔進了第四號病房，發現一個似乎是年輕的男人躺在一張病床上，頭部已經被一張白色的床單蓋上了，表示這個病人已經死了。同時，他也聽到那個護士在電話中將這個不幸的消息通知什麼人。

Tai-lin was ecstatic. He rushed to Unit Four and discovered a seemingly young man lying on a bed with a white sheet covering his head indicating that the patient had died. And he heard the nurse on the phone telling someone about the sad news.

這正是他所要尋找的！沒有任何猶豫，泰林向著這死亡的病人衝去，擠進了屍體。霎那間，他睜開了他的眼睛，用手將白色的床單從頭上拉了下來。

It was exactly what he was looking for! Without any hesitation, Tai-lin rushed toward the dead patient and squeezed himself into the corpse. In another second, he opened his eyes, reached up and pulled down the white bed sheet from his head.

就在這個時候，一個年齡較長的女護士走進了房間。當她發現這個已經被宣佈死亡的男子正茫然地坐在床上時，她大為震驚。

Just at that moment, an older female nurse came into the room. When she saw the declared dead man sitting up on the bed, she was shocked and confused.

"這個死人活了回來了！" 她驚駭不已，尖銳地叫道。
"The dead man has revived!" she screamed, astonished.

立刻，所有的醫護人員都衝進四號病房，每個人都認為這是奇跡簡直不可思議。

Soon all of the other medical staff rushed into the Unit Four, and everybody was amazed at the apparent miracle.

第七章　Chapter Seven

看到了這麼多的醫生和護士圍繞著他，泰林明瞭了這是怎麼的一回事了。他很興奮他終於又變成了一個人了，可是，當他注視他的手和腿時，他知道他已經犯了一個很大的錯誤，他選擇了一個不是中國人而是個外國人的屍體。

Seeing so many doctors and nurses surrounding him, Tai-lin realized what had happened. He was excited for he had finally become a human again. But when he looked at his hands and legs, he knew he had made a great mistake. He had chosen the dead body of a foreign man instead of a Chinese one.

因為每一個人都叫他 Cubin 先生，他知道那是他的，不，是這個死者的姓氏，可他還不知道這個外國人的名字是什麼，他也不知道這個外國人是從那一個國家來的。他不能否認他是個外國人，也不能承認他是個中國人，所以他什麼也不說，任憑醫務人員的一切安排，他緊口不語，當人們接近他時，他就對著這個人微笑。

As everybody called him Mr. Cubin, he knew it must be his, no, the dead man's last name, yet he did not know what the foreign man's first name was, and he did not know which country the foreigner came from. He could not deny he was a foreigner, and he could not admit he was a Chinese either. He said nothing, but let the medical staff arrange everything for him. He kept his mouth shut but smiled at everyone who approached him.

　　第二天下午他辦理出院手續。因爲他要在醫院的文件中簽字，他終於明瞭了他的全名 James W. Cubin 及他目前住在成都市一家最豪華的五星級飯店黃龍賓館，他的出生年月日是一九八一年六月十日，這就是說他今年二十三歲。

He was discharged next day afternoon. From the hospital papers he was asked to sign, he finally realized that his full name was James W. Cubin and he currently stayed at Yellow Dragon Inn, the most luxurious five-star hotel in Chen-du City. His birth date was June 10, 1981. It meant that he was 23 years old.

　　當他在簽他的名字時，他聽到人們用中國話耳語這個外國人怎麼沒有死啊。一個年老的婦人大聲地說，當然仍是中文，"我知道的，因爲我是佛教徒。這是閻羅王的士兵弄錯了的。根據閻羅王府的生死簿，這個人不應當這麼年輕就死亡的。當冥府官員發現這個錯誤時，他們就把他的靈魂送還了他的身體。一切就是這麼樣的簡單。"

When he was signing his name, he heard people around him whisper to each other in Chinese that the foreigner had not really been dead. One old woman said loudly, in Chinese of course, "I know it because I'm a Buddhist. It was a mistake the Hades' soldiers had made. According to the records of life and death in Hades' office, the man should not have died so young. When the ghost government officials found the mistake, they sent the man's soul back to his body. That's so simple."

泰林如何去回答這些說法？他假裝他是一個外國人，當然聽不懂中國話。

How could Tai-lin react to the saying? He pretended that being a foreigner he did not understand the Chinese language anyway.

醫院裡一個服務人員爲他叫了一部計程車，他被帶回了黃龍賓館。賓館裡的人員看到他回來了都很興奮，一個年輕男子把他帶到 "他的" 房間，第 1683 號房。

One of the hospital staff called a taxi for him and he was taken back to Yellow Dragon Inn. Upon seeing him back, the hotel employees were all excited and one young man immediately ushered him to "his" assigned room, number 1683.

當這個男子走了後，他關上了房門並又把門鎖了。他開始搜查 James 留在房間裡的所有物品。他找到了很多文件及一本美國護照，原來他是一個美國公民。文件上說他來自科羅拉多州丹佛市，可他對科羅拉多州是個什麼地方毫無所知，因為他從來沒有聽說過這個地方。他知道在這個時候，不管他想如何地去向他週圍的人們解釋說他不是 James W. Cubin，而是一個名字叫蔡泰林的中國人，那是沒有一個人會相信他的話的，反而因此會使他陷入更為混亂的處境，及造成事件的加倍困難和複雜性。所以他決定什麼也不說，而且也不再說中國話，只說他當年在成衣工廠英文班上所學得的簡單英語。

Soon after the man left, Tai-lin closed the door and locked it. He started to search for what James had left in the room. He found many documents and a US passport. So the foreigner was a citizen of the United States. The documents listed that James was from Denver, Colorado, but Tai-lin had no idea where Colorado was, as he had never heard of such a place. He knew by this time, no matter how much he tried to explain to the people around him that he was not James W. Cubin, but a Chinese man named Tai-lin Cai, nobody would believe him and that would definitely put him in a much more confused and awkward situation and create many difficult and complicated problems. So he decided to say nothing and he would not speak Chinese anymore but rather the simple English he had learned from the English class at the garment factory.

在 James 的物品中，他又找到了一個大信封裡面有八千九百美元的一家美國銀行簽發的旅行支票。信封上有 James 的名字及地址。他知道這一定是 James 在美國的家中地址。

同時，他又發現了好幾封信件。顯然的，那些都是 James 的父母親及他的兄弟們寫給他的信件，信封上都註明發自丹佛。很奇怪，他就是找不到關於 James 的妻子及孩子們的資訊。*James 還是單身嗎？*他無法證實。

In James' belongings, he also found a large envelope and inside of the envelope there were many traveler checks issued by an American bank totaling eight thousand and nine hundred dollars. On the envelope there were James' name and an address. He knew that the address must be James' home in the United States. He also discovered several old letters. Obviously, they were mailed to James by his parents and brothers. The letters were all addressed from Denver. Strangely enough, he did not find any information about James' wife or children. *Was James single?* He had no way to confirm.

在收集了關於 James 的所有資訊後，他坐在一張椅子上思考著下一步該怎麼走。

After having collected all of the information regarding James, Tai-lin sat on a chair meditating about what to do next.

首先，關於這個美國男子 James W. Cubin，他還有很多沒有答案的問題。

First, he still had many unanswered questions about this American man, James W. Cubin.

*爲什麼 James 被送到急診室？是什麼導致他死亡的？他爲什麼來到中國，是商業還是私人旅行？如果是商業，那他經營什麼行業？如果是私人，那又是爲什麼？文件上面說他的家人都住在丹佛，不知道都是些什麼樣的人？*雖然他沒有發現任何關於 James 的妻子或孩子的資訊，從他的年齡上看來，James 可能早已經結婚了及有很多的孩子。*如果是的，不知道他的妻子叫什麼名字，及長相如何？他究竟有幾個孩子？他們的年齡多大了？*

Why was James sent to an emergency room? What caused his death? Why did he come to China, on business, or for a private reason? If on business, what kind of business did he have? If on a private reason, what was it? The papers said that his family all lived in Denver. What kind of people were they? Although he did not find any information about James' wife or children, from his age, James might be married and have children. *If so, what was his wife's name and what did she look like? And how many children did he have? How old were they?*

他坐在椅子上繼續不停地想著這些問題，可是他找不到任何一個答案。

He sat on a chair, continued to contemplate these questions but he could not uncover any one of the answers.

接著，他的最緊急的問題必須處理：*我應該留在中國這個我出生的國家嗎？可是，中國不是 James 的國家。James*

*的國家是美國，可那不是我的國家。我能依照我的希望及蘋蘋所說只要我復活了她就嫁給我而應當去和她結婚嗎？*再一細思，他明瞭了他是不能如此去做的，因為他現在不是泰林了而是一個外國人，他甚至於連他自己究竟是誰也不清楚，他怎麼可以企盼蘋蘋去嫁給如此一個完全陌生的外國男子？

Then, his most urgent questions came to his mind: *Should I stay in China, the country I was born? But China is not James' country. James' country is the United States, but that is not my country. Should I go to Pin-pin and marry her as I had wished and she had said she would if I were revived?* But on a second thought, he realized he could not do it now, as he was not Tai-lin but a foreigner. He even did not know who he was. How could he expect Pin-pin to marry such a totally unknown foreign man?

那我應該到那裡去及我的下一步又將如何去做？
Then where I should go and what should I do?

他對這些問題完全找不到答案，就連一個答案也沒有！而那最糟糕的是在這世界上他沒有一個人可問或者商量。當吃晚飯的時間到了，他仍是一片茫然。因為肚子餓了，乃到餐廳去吃飯。

He had no answers to any of those questions, not even a single one! And the worst thing was that in the whole world he had nobody to ask, or to consult. When the time for supper came, he still had not found a way out. As he was hungry, he went to the dining room to eat.

在一間豪華的旅館餐廳裡，他被帶到一個座位上坐下了。一個中國女侍微笑地歡迎他，用著生硬的英語問他是否仍像以往一樣地要份紐約牛排或者 T 形牛排。泰林糊塗了，他從來沒有吃過什麼牛排，對於這些食物他一無所知。他搖搖頭指著菜單上的一道中國菜。這一次，輪到女侍糊塗了，*怎麼這次這個外國人改變他最喜歡吃的食物了？*

He was seated in a luxurious hotel's dining room. A smiling Chinese waitress greeted him and asked him in broken English if he would still like to order a New York sirloin or T-bone steak as usual. Tai-lin was confused. He had never eaten the so-called steaks, and he had no idea what they were. He shook his head but pointed to a Chinese dish on the menu. This time, the waitress became confused. *Why did the foreigner change the selection of his favorite food this time?*

晚飯後，他回到他的房間，仍在思索著他的下一步該怎麼走。最後他決定他必須儘快離開中國到美國去會見 James 的家人，雖然他知道當他到達 James 的家後那又將帶給他另一連串的煩惱，可是他想他已經別無選擇了。

After supper, he went back to his room, still thinking about what he should do next. Finally, he decided that he must leave China for the United States to meet James' family as soon as possible, although he knew he would face another series of problems when returning to James' home. But he believed he had no choice.

　　第二天，他要求旅館裡的一個人員幫他買了一張回去美國的機票，這個人告訴他當他被發現在旅館外面吃了什麼海鮮中毒時，大家都害怕得要死，幸運地他現在平安無事了。他問泰林那究竟是怎麼一回事，及他在什麼地方吃的有毒的海鮮？

The next day, when he asked a hotel clerk to buy an airplane ticket for him to return America, the clerk told him that when he was discovered of being poisoned after eating some kind of fancy seafood outside of the hotel, everybody was scared to death. Luckily, he was all right now. He asked Tai-lin what had happened to him, and where he had eaten the poisoned seafood?

　　*我究竟發生了什麼事？*泰林沒有回答任何一個問題，僅尷尬地笑著說了聲 "謝謝" ，這個人也沒有注意到他的尷尬笑容。

What happened to me? Tai-lin did not answer any of the questions, but said "Thank you" with an embarrassing smile, which the clerk did not notice.

　　機票到手後，他飛回了美國，這個在他今後的歲月中必須承認的母國。

With airplane ticket in hand, he flew back to the United States, the nation he would have to claim as his mother country in the years ahead.

第八章　Chapter Eight

當泰林看見一位六十多歲已有灰色頭髮的年長男子來應門時，他明瞭這個男子一定是 James 的父親，乃立刻以那外國腔調英語叫了聲 "爸"。老人對於他兒子的突然出現感到詫異，因而沒有注意到他的外國口音英語，僅責問他為什麼不先打個電話回家好讓他和他的母親去機場接他。然後大聲地向著裡面叫道，"*親愛的，出來看誰回來了！*"

When Tai-lin saw a gray-haired man in his mid-sixties answer the door, he realized that the man must be James' father. He immediately called him "Dad" in English tainted by his foreign accent. The older man was so surprised at his son's sudden appearance that he did not seem to notice the accented English, but blamed him for not calling home first so he and his mother could pick him up at the airport. Then he loudly yelled to the inside of house, "*Honey, come and see who is back?*"

立刻一位年長婦人衝了出來，她一把緊緊地抱住泰林，並在他的兩邊臉上用力地親吻個不停。泰林從來沒有接受過如此的美國式家人熱情，他感覺很是不安。

Soon a senior woman rushed out. She hugged Tai-lin tightly and kissed him on his both cheeks again and again. Tai-lin had never experienced the American way of showing family affection. He felt very uneasy.

他們走進客廳坐下了。在這對老夫婦還沒有對他的旅行發出任何問話前，泰林站了起來，以最嚴肅的態度聲明著說，"我很抱歉，我必須告訴你們，我不是你們的兒子 James。我是一個中國男子名叫蔡泰林。"

They walked into the living room and sat down. Before the senior couple could ask him any further questions about his trip, Tai-lin stood up and exclaimed in the most serious way he could, "I'm sorry I have to tell you that I'm not your son, James. I am a Chinese man named Tai-lin Cai."

他就如何向 James 的家人以英語解釋他的情況籌思已久，他知道他不能隱瞞真象。他告訴自己*實話實說應該是對付目前情況的唯一途徑*。至於他將又會面臨著什麼樣的的後果，他已經顧不得了。

He had thought for a long time about how to explain his situation in English when he met James' family. He knew he could not hide the truth. *Telling the truth should be the only way to face a situation like this,* he told himself. As for what consequences he might face, he simply did not care anymore.

"*再說一次，*"兩位老人幾乎立刻同時地命令道，因為他們不能確定他們剛才所聽到的。

"*Say that again,*" the two seniors demanded immediately almost at the same time for they were not uncertain of what they had just heard.

"*我的身體屬於你們兒子的，可我是一個中國幽靈，在你們的兒子死了後，我借用了他的屍體復活了。你們的兒子已經在中國死亡了。*"泰林儘可能地緩慢清楚地敘說。

"*My body belongs to your son, but I'm a Chinese spirit. I borrowed your son's body to be revived after his death. Your son has died in China.*" Tai-lin spoke very slowly and tried to be as clear as he could.

終於，這對老人似乎明瞭他所說的事情了，可是他們不能相信他的話語。這對可憐的老人相互告訴對方 James 一定得了一種奇怪的神智失常症。

Finally, the older couple seemed to understand what he had said, but they could not believe his words. The poor old couple told each other that James must have suffered a strange mental disorder.

於是，這個年老的男子又問他，"*告訴我這究竟是怎麼一回事，愈詳細愈好。*"

Then the old man asked him again, "*Tell me what*

happened to you as much details as possible."

　　泰林乃儘其全力用他那破爛的英文告訴這對夫婦他原來是誰，及他如何借用 James 的身體來還陽爲人。可是事實上，不管他如何解釋，這對老夫婦就是不能相信如此一個奇怪神秘的故事，因爲他們一生中從來沒有聽過這麼一個說法。老人與他的妻子商量了一下，他們決定先讓他們的 "兒子" 好好地吃一頓飯，然後把他送回 "他的" 臥房，使他睡個好覺。他們想，*也許第二天情況便會不一樣了。*

As much as he could, Tai-lin used his broken English to tell the couple who he was originally and how he borrowed James' body to revive as a human again. But the fact was that no matter how much he tried to explain it, the senior couple just could not believe such a strange and mysterious story, as they had never heard of it in their lives. The old man consulted with his wife. They decided to feed their "son" a good meal first then put him back to "his" bedroom to let him have a good rest. *Maybe the next day, things would be different,* they hoped.

　　可是第二天早上，他們的兒子仍然和前一天一模一樣。他們乃急忙電話他們的友人醫生，中西部數州最有名的精神科醫生，Dr. Bill Castrow，並訂了個緊急約會，帶著他們的兒子去看這位專科醫生。

But the next morning, their son was still the same as that of the day before. They hurriedly called and made an urgent appointment with their friend doctor, Dr. Bill Castrow, the most well known psychiatrist in the Midwest States, and took their son to see the specialist.

　　仔細地檢查了以後，Dr. Castrow 也找不出這個年輕人的毛病究竟是什麼，不過他肯定地認為 James 是害了一種嚴重的精神病。他告訴這對夫婦他必須將他們的兒子送入醫院內長期觀察和治療。

After careful examination, Dr. Castrow could not tell what was wrong with this young man, but he was sure that James had developed a serious psychiatric problem. He told the couple that he must put their son in a hospital for a long-term observation and treatment.

　　於是泰林（James）住進了科羅拉多州最好的精神病醫院 First Denver Memorial Hospital。不久，James 的兩個哥哥及他們的妻子都到醫院裡看望他們的小兄弟，泰林開始認識及記憶他的每一位美國親人的姓名及容貌。

Tai-lin（James）was admitted to First Denver Memorial Hospital, the best one for psychiatric patients in Colorado. Soon afterward, James' two brothers and their wives all came to the hospital to visit their youngest brother. Tai-lin started to learn and remember the names and faces of each of his American relatives.

　　慢慢地他知道了 James W. Cubin 的家世了。他是他父母的最小的孩子。他的父親 Joel Cubin 是丹佛市 Cubin Homebuilder Company 的創辦人及董事長。母親 Sue Cubin 是個中學教師。他們有三個孩子，都是男孩。James 的兩個哥哥都是他們父親公司裡的的副董事長，一位負責建築工程，一位負責財務。James 於一年前畢業於丹佛大學主修宗教及哲學。畢業後，他的父親安排他在家庭公司裡做辦公室主任。

　　Gradually, he learned the background of James W. Cubin. He was the youngest child of his parents. His father, Joel Cubin, was the founder and president of Cubin Homebuilder Company in Denver. His mother, Sue Cubin, was a high school teacher. They had three children, all boys. James' two elder brothers worked for their father as vice presidents. One was in charge of construction and the other one was in charge of financial affairs. James graduated from University of Denver a year earlier, majoring in religion and philosophy. After graduation, his father arranged for him to work for their family business as the the director of administration.

　　六個月後，Joel 和 Sue 都提早退休了。Joel 把公司裡的業務都交給三個兒子負責，James 的大哥 George 擔任董事長，二哥 Henry 為第一副董事長仍然負責財務。James 對於建築業沒有多大的興趣，就喜歡到世界上那些古老國家如中國、埃及、印度等處去旅遊。他要求他的父母及哥哥們讓他先暢快地環遊世界一週，然後回來專心工作。

Six months later, Joel and Sue both took early retirement. Joel let his three sons take over the company business. James' eldest brother, George, became president and the second elder brother, Henry, the first senior vice president still in charge of financial affairs. James was not interested in the construction business, but longed to travel to some ancient nations such as China, Egypt, and India. He asked his parents and brothers to let him travel around the world first then come back to concentrate on his work.

他有一個女朋友 Susan Ford，他大學裡的同班同學。因為他經常長期到國外旅遊而她最討厭到外國去只喜歡停留在美國國內，他們的親密關係終於終止了。這以後，他沒有興趣再去接交新的女友，放心地去從事他的旅遊了。

He had a girlfriend, Susan Ford, who was his classmate in college. Due to his frequent and lengthy travels abroad while she hated to go to foreign nations but liked to stay in the United States, their intimate relationship finally ended. After that, he had no interest in looking for a new girlfriend, but wished to travel more often.

首先，他跟隨丹佛市一家旅行社主辦的兩週中國旅遊團去中國玩了一次，回來後，他又單獨一人回去中國。他告訴家人他計劃這次在這個擁有古老文化的中國停留三個月，也許更長。

First, he took a quick two-week tour of China with a Denver travel agency's tourist group. After that, he came back to China on his own. He told his family that he planned to stay in the old civilized nation, China, for three months this time, maybe longer.

現在，只有一個半月後，他就回家了，而且說他不是 James，是一個中國人。當然啦，沒有人相信他，因為沒有人會相信一個精神病人的故事。於是他繼續被留在醫院裡。

Now, only one and half months later, he returned home, saying that he was not James but a Chinese! Naturally, nobody believed him, as nobody believed a psychiatric patient's story. So he remained in the hospital.

這項安排對於泰林來說，真是有意料之外的喜悅，因為時間可以使他熟悉他的完全 "新" 的國家，他的 "新" 的家人，以及 "新" 的風俗和習慣，甚至於最普通的美國速食漢堡和皮薩，他也必須學習享受。

For Tai-lin, he was unexpectedly happy with the arrangement, for time would let him become familiar with his totally "new" nation and his "new" family, as well as all of the "new" customs and traditions. Even the most common American fast foods, hamburger and pizza, he had to learn to appreciate.

現在，他有充足的時間去學習英文，他的英文進步很快，因爲他每天必須和醫院裡的人員、其他的病人、以及那所有環繞在他身邊的人用英語會話。他儘全力去學習他的"外國"語文，一年後，他的日常生活英文會話已經說得很流暢了。

Now he had plenty of time to learn English. His English improved rapidly due to the daily conversation with the hospital employees, the other patients, and all the other people around him. He studied his "foreign" language as hard as he could. A year later, he spoke everyday English very well.

第九章　Chapter Nine

Donna Jones 是個有執照的護士，在泰林住的醫院裡工作。她是第三代冰島移民，從和 James 的父母談話中，她明瞭 Joel 是第二代冰島移民，而 James 就是和她一樣第三代冰島移民了。在丹佛的冰島移民並不是很多，她感覺到她和 James 這家人的血族關係應該很親近，因而也開始對泰林特別注意，她感覺這個病人很正常，和其他的精神病人不同。同時，她也奇怪怎麼一個第三代移民的英語還說得像個外國人。她不敢問他，如果她問，她知道他一定會告訴她他那個無法使人相信的故事，他不是美國人而是個中國人。她明瞭作爲一個護士，她是不可以去碰那些碰不得的問題的。所以對於泰林的英語，她閉口不問了。

Donna Jones was a registered nurse who worked at the

hospital where Tai-lin was a patient. She was a third generation Icelandic immigrant. From James' parents' conversation she realized that Joel was a second generation Icelandic immigrant and James was a third generation like her. Since there were not many Icelandic immigrants in Denver, she felt a close kinship with James' family. She started to pay attention to Tai-lin, and found that the patient was very normal, not like the other psychiatric patients. Meanwhile, she wondered how a third generation immigrant spoke English like a foreigner. She dared not ask him. If she did, she knew he would tell her his most unbelievable story again that he was not an American but a Chinese. She realized that as a nurse, she was not supposed to touch the untouchable issues. So she remained mute as far as Tai-lin's English was concerned.

一天，Donna 無意中發現 James 對醫院裡娛樂室中的乒乓球檯子似乎很有興趣，她問他是否知道如何打乒乓球，因為她很喜歡這種運動，當年她在大學讀書時就是學校裡的乒乓球代表隊隊員，而且是絕頂高手之一。

One day, Donna happened to discover that James seemed to be interested in the ping pong table in the hospital recreation room. She asked him if he knew how to play table tennis, as she was very fond of the sport. When she was a nursing student in the college; she was a member of the school's ping pong team and was one of best players.

　　泰林的回答出乎她的意料，他向她挑戰五局。她去問醫院裡的領導在她不上班的時候可否和這個病人 James 打乒乓球。在獲得准許後，Donna 和泰林打乒乓球，結果五局全輸給了泰林，而且整整打了一個下午，她連一局也沒有贏過！她大為驚訝。於是，泰林告訴她，他是中國成都市裡的乒乓球冠軍。Donna 笑著沒有答他的話。

　　Unexpectedly, Tai-lin challenged her to play a five game set against him. She went to see the hospital administrator inquiring if she could play ping pong with the patient, James, on her day off. With permission, Donna played table tennis with Tai-lin, and she lost all of the five games. And for the whole afternoon, she did not even win a single game! She was embarrassed and amazed. Then Tai-lin told her that he was the ping pong champion in his city, Chen-du, China. Donna laughed but said nothing.

　　*莫非他真是如他自己所說的是個中國人？*Donna 自言自語道。

　　Is he really a Chinese as he claimed? Donna asked herself.

　　即使如此，Donna 仍然相信除了他喜歡編造自己的故事外，這個病人委實沒有一點兒精神病。

　　Even so, Donna still believed that the patient had no mental problems at all, except for the strange story he liked to create about himself.

　　因爲有了打乒乓球的同一個興趣，這兩個年輕人，一個護士和她的病人，很快建立了友誼。

　　Because of the same interest in table tennis, a friendship soon arose between the two young people, a nurse and her patient.

　　泰林逐漸明瞭了想使別人相信他的故事是絕對不可能的，因此，當再有人問及他的背景時，他絕口不提了。他的英語進步得很快，除非是談專門性的問題，他已經可以和人談得頭頭是道而像個"真正"的美國人。如果人們不知道他自己編造的故事及不太注意他那含有外國腔調的英語，沒有人會懷疑他不是個真正的美國人。

　　Gradually, Tai-lin realized that it was absolutely impossible to make other people believe his story, so he kept his mouth shut whenever he was asked about his background. As his English was rapidly improving, he could converse with people as normally as a "true" American if the subject was not too specific. By this time, if people did not know his imaginative story and did not pay much attention to his foreign-accented English, no one would doubt he was not American.`

　　他來自富裕的家庭，受過大學教育，行爲端正，人們對他的印象很好，他和別人也相處得很愉快。一年後，他被告知可以出院了，回到他的家庭事業工作，他的兩個哥哥安排他爲第二副董事長。

He was from a wealthy family, with a college degree, and displayed good behavior. Everybody treated him nicely. He got along with others very well. A year later, he was discharged from the hospital and went back to work for his family business. His two elder brothers put him back to work as second vice president.

　　他和 Donna 一有時間就去一家體育俱樂部打乒乓球。打完了球，他往往就會請她在他們兩人都喜歡的一家高級義大利飯店裡用餐。除了打乒乓球外，他們兩人也喜歡跳舞，經常去一家一般年輕戀人們常去的舞廳裡跳。他們的約會日益頻繁，最後幾乎每天晚間都要見面。

He and Donna still played ping pong at a sport club whenever they had time. After playing, he often invited her to eat at a fancy Italian restaurant they both loved. Besides ping pong, they also enjoyed dancing and often danced at a night dancing hall where many young lovers went. Their dates became more frequent that gradually developing to meeting each other every evening.

　　在一個下雨的夜晚，他留她在他家過夜，他的家是棟新建的三個臥房的房子，是他們家庭公司建造的，他的兩個哥哥送給他的禮品。天色晚了，他請 Donna 去另一個臥房休息。Donna 向他望了下，嘴角含羞地拉著他的手，給了他一個深深的吻，然後在他的耳邊問他，"*你願意和我做愛嗎？*"
"*我當然願意，*" 泰林興奮地回答。

One late rainy night, he kept her at his home, a brand-new
3-bedroom house, built by his family's company and presented
to him as a gift by his two elder brothers. He asked Dnna to take
one of the other two bedrooms when the time was late. Donna
looked at him, a coy smile playing at her mouth. She grabbed
his hands and pulled him to her. She kissed him long and hard
then whispered in his ear, "*Would you like to make love to me?*"
"*I would love to,*" Tai-lin replied excitedly.

於是他將她帶到他的臥房，他們脫光了衣服。泰林回想
起他和織成在天堂裡做愛時的種種快樂經驗，他和 Donna 雙
雙躺在床上，靜靜地相互望著對方，他們的手慢慢地撫摸著
對方的赤裸身體，他們接吻，他們愛撫，終於 Donna 將泰林
拉上她的身體，輕柔地對他說，"*請輕點兒，親愛的。*"
"*我會的，*" 泰林愉快地答允。

Then he led her to his bedroom and they undressed. Tai-lin
recalled how pleasures an experience it had been when he and
Ze-chen had made love in Heaven. He and Donna stretched out
along each other on the bed and quietly looked into each other's
eyes and their hands slowly moved along the other's bare skin.
They kissed and fondled more frequently until Donna pulled
Tai-lin on top of her and said softly, "*Be gentle, dear.*"
"*I will,*" Tai-lin joyfully promised.

做完了愛後，他們躺在床上休息，泰林向 Donna 求婚，Donna 沒有太多考慮就答允了。一個月後，他們在他們的家庭教堂丹佛的 Alameda Hills Baptist Church 舉行了結婚典禮，兩家的家人親戚和一些好友們包括泰林以前的精神科醫生 Dr. Bill Castrow 都參加了他們的婚禮。

After making love, they rested on the bed. Then Tai-lin asked Donna to marry him. Donna accepted without much consideration. A month later, they married at their family church, Alameda Hills Baptist Church in Denver, witnessed and blessed by both of their families, relatives, and some close friends, including Dr. Bill Castrow, Tai-lin's former psychiatric doctor.

婚後他們去歐洲度蜜月。蜜月歸來後不久，泰林就發現他又犯了一個大錯了，就好像當初他急於借屍還魂時，他沒有找到中國人而借用了一個外國人的屍體。作為朋友或情人，他和 Donna 相處得很好，而且他們又都很愛對方；然而作為夫妻，他們就不能像美國新婚夫婦一樣地快樂了。他是個道道地地的中國人不管他如何長得像美國人。他的中國生活方式與 Donna 的西方生活方式是不能相融的。

After returning from their honeymoon in Europe, Tai-lin soon found that he had made a great mistake again like that when he wanted to be revived, he took a foreigner's dead body instead of a Chinese's. Being friends or lovers, he and Donna got along very well, and they loved each other very much, but being a married couple, they could not live together as happily as a newly married American couple. He was practically a Chinese no matter how much he looked like an American. His Chinese philosophy just could not match Donna's Western style.

他們開始爲一些小事爭論，然後又爲生活的方式而大起爭吵。慢慢地，Donna 開始懷疑她的丈夫 James W. Cubin 是否真如他自己以前所說的是個中國人而不是美國人。如同其他的一些美國夫妻一樣，他們在結婚半年後就訴諸離婚了。雙方並沒有作很多的惡意批評，對多數的人來說，結婚是相互瞭解的結果，但是，對於泰林和 Donna 而言，相互瞭解的結果是離婚。

They started to argue over some small things first, then the basic way of living. Gradually, Donna began to doubt if her husband, James W. Cubin, was really an American or a Chinese as he had claimed before. Like many other couples in the United States, they filed for divorce half a year after they were married. They did not criticize each other too much. For the most couples, marriage was the product of understanding each other, but for Tai-lin and Donna, the product of understanding each other was a divorce.

離婚後，他們仍然相互關懷，仍然有時候在一起打乒乓球或跳舞，不過不像以往那樣的親密或頻繁吧了，他們維持著良好的友誼。當然，他們也不再住在同一棟房子裡面，也不在一起做愛了。

After their divorce, they still cared about each other, and played ping pong or danced once in a while like friends but not as intimately or frequently as before. They maintained a good friendship. Of course, they did not live under one roof anymore, nor did they ever make love again.

泰林恢復了他的獨身生活。沒有 Donna 的日夜在身邊，他突然感覺寂寞，不過同時，他也感到一種解脫，天天吃中國飯，讀中國書，聽中國的音樂，完全像個中國人，不過是住在新大陸，這個他根本就從來沒有接受過的國家。他開始非常懷念他的母國，中國。

Tai-lin returned to his bachelor life. Without Donna by his side day and night, loneliness was his new constant companion. However, he was glad to be relieved in one way or the other, eating the Chinese food, reading the Chinese books, listening to the Chinese music, acting totally as a Chinese every day but in the new land, which he never wanted to claim as his own country. He started to miss his mother country, China, very much.

一天，他在丹佛郵報上看到了一隻簡短新聞說，中國成都發生大火把一家成衣工廠完全燒燬了，很多員工都葬身火場。新聞報導中並沒有提及這家工廠的名字，突然間，他想起了蘋蘋，他的初戀，多年前曾為她自殺的中國女孩。

One day, he read a brief news report in the Denver Post saying that a big fire destroyed a garment factory in Chen-Du, China killing many employees. But the news report did not mention the name of factory. Suddenly, he thought of Pin-pin, his first love, the girl for whom he had died years ago.

*不知道這家工廠是不是我曾經在那裡工作過的康復成衣工廠？如果是的，不知道蘋蘋是否在死亡的名單中？*他自問著，可是沒有人可以回答他。而這個問題每天都在困擾著他，終於，他決定飛到成都去找尋答案。因為聖誕節假期即將來到，他又向公司裡請了五天假，如此一來，他就可以在中國停留一個星期了。

Was this the Comfort Garment Factory I used to work in? If it is, is Pin-pin on the list of dead employees? He asked, but nobody could answer for him. As the question kept tormenting him daily, finally, he decided to fly to Chen-Du to find the answers. As the Christmas holidays were coming, he asked for five additional days leave so he could spend a week in China.

第十章 Chapter Ten

泰林到達了成都。不久，他就如釋重負地發現康復成衣工廠仍在經營著，明顯地沒有受到一點損害，那是另一家規模較大可也很陳舊的成衣工廠，它已經完全燒燬了。

Tai-lin arrived in Chen-Du. Soon he was relieved to find

that Comfort Garment Factory was still operating, apparently without any damage. It was another garment factory, a bigger one but much older, which had been totally burned down.

是一個很晚的下午,他回到了康復成衣工廠,斯時正是員工們下班回家的時候。因為他現在是個外國人了,他不適宜站在工廠的大門口,或者去特別訊問一個女性員工,所以他站在一段距離之外望著那成百的男男女女走出了工廠。

He returned to Comfort Garment Factory in a late afternoon. It was the time for the employees to leave for home. As he was now a foreigner, it would not be suitable for him to stand at the factory's front entrance or to ask for a specific female employee, so he simply stood at a distance, watching hundreds of men and women walking out of the factory.

不管泰林是如何仔細地觀望,他就是沒有發現蘋蘋在這些員工中。那這是不是說她已經去了美國?他無法求證他的猜測。

As carefully as he watched, he did not find Pin-pin among the employees. Did it mean that she had already left for the United States? He had no way to confirm his suspicion.

不久,是晚餐的時間到了,他感覺到飢餓。於是走到附近一家他和蘋蘋以前經常光顧過的小飯店。他計劃先用一頓速食,然後再決定下一步如何走。

Soon it was the time for supper and he felt hungry. He walked to a small restaurant nearby, where he and Pin-pin had often eaten before. He planned to have a quick meal, then, decide what he should do next.

他選擇了餐廳後面一角的一個雙人座位，那是他和蘋蘋以往常坐的地方。像以往一樣，他叫了他最喜歡吃的牛肉抄飯，外加兩條春捲及一碗青菜豆腐湯。

He took a booth at a corner in the back of the dining room where he and Pin-pin used to sit. As he often did before, he ordered his favorite dishes, beef fried rice, two egg rolls and a bowl of tofu and vegetable soup.

當他低著頭喝湯時，他注意到有個人向著他的方向移動。抬頭一望，他驚喜萬分地發現蘋蘋正朝著他走來。當然，她是不可能認識這個在她面前的外國男子是她以前的中國愛人。明顯地，她正在尋找她的老位子。因為泰林佔了，她乃坐在他的鄰桌旁椅子上。不久，她又奇怪地發現這個外國人不僅佔了她的老位子，同時也在吃著他以前男朋友最喜歡吃的東西，這真是太湊巧了！

As he was lowering his head to drink the soup, he noticed a person moving toward his direction. Lifting his head, he was happily surprised to find Pin-pin walking toward him. Of course, she could not recognize that the foreign man in front of her was her former Chinese lover. Obviously, out of habit she was looking for her old seat. Since Tai-lin took it, she sat at the table next to his. Soon, she was interested to find that the foreigner not only took her old seat but also was eating the same kind of dishes as her former lover used to order. What a strange coincidence!

可能是利用這個機會去練習她的新的外國語言，她不經意地向泰林用她那帶有濃厚外國腔調的英語說了聲 "Hi"。這聲招呼使得泰林大為興奮，因為他正在為如何接近她發愁。於是他立刻回答了聲 "Hi" 並附帶一個友誼的微笑。然後他們開始交談了。在他們的飯還沒有吃完前，他們已經快速建立起了友誼。

Perhaps taking advantage of an opportunity to practice her new language, she casually said "Hi" to Tai-lin in her strong-accented English. The address made Tai-lin overjoyed, as he had not yet figured out a way how to approach her. He quickly replied "Hi" together with a friendly smile. Then, they started to talk. Before their meals were finished, they had built a quick friendship.

當泰林發現蘋蘋不能夠完全明瞭他的英語時，他就故意在他的話語中混雜著一些美國腔調的中國話。在談話中，泰林知道了蘋蘋還是非常強烈地希望能去美國。她也知道由於美國移民局尚不發給中國人旅遊簽証，她是無法申請到正式的美國簽証的。然而，她仍然不放棄她的美國夢，因為有很多和她一樣背景的中國人民都能夠找到方法去了美國。

When Tai-lin found Pin-pin could not fully understand his English, he purposely mixed some American-accented Chinese words in his conversation. During the talk, he learned that she was still very much interested in going to the United States. She had realized she was not qualified to apply for a regular visa for there was no tourist visa to be issued by the American immigration office to a Chinese citizen. Yet she did not want to give up her American dream either, because many other Chinese people with the similar backgrounds as hers had found their ways to go to the United States.

她的朋友的朋友，那個以前曾經邀請她和她同去美國的女子早已經又去了美國，據說她最近已與住在紐約的一個富有的美籍中國男子結婚了，現在，她已有美國的永久居留證，合法地和她的丈夫居住在一棟豪華的房子裡。凡是認識她的人都羨慕她的好運。蘋蘋告訴這個外國人（泰林）她希望將來也能有這個好運。

Her friend's friend, the woman who invited her to go to America with her before, had gone to the United States again. And it was said that she had recently married a wealthy Chinese man in New York City who was a naturalized US citizen. Now she had an American permanent resident card and legally lived at a luxurious house with her husband. Everybody who knew her envied her. Pin-pin told the foreigner（Tai-lin）she wished to have the same good luck one of these days.

當她發現這個年輕的美國人 James 是單身，很喜歡中國文化及中國烹飪，她半開玩笑地問他是否也喜歡中國的女孩子？泰林豎起他的大拇指模仿外國人說中國話，"頂好"，意思就是非常好。

When she learned that the young American man, James, was single and very fond of the Chinese culture and Chinese food, she asked him half jokingly how about the Chinese girls? Tai-lin thumbed up imitating a foreigner's speaking Chinese, "Ding Hao" which literally meant super good.

這兩個字回答使得蘋蘋非常興奮。她突然有了一個奇怪的想法，如果她能嫁給 James，她就是美國公民的配偶，而可以得到簽証去到美國合法地居住在那裡，和她住在紐約的朋友一樣地快樂，這真是一個快速而又合法的途徑去實現她那多年的美國夢！

The two-word reply made Pin-pin excited. She suddenly had a strange idea. If she could marry James, she would become an American citizen's spouse and could get a visa to go and stay in the United States legally and happily like her friend's friend in New York City. This was indeed a fast and legal way to materialize her years of dreaming to go to America!

她愈想就愈是興奮。但是，這個美國人說他在中國的假期只有五天了，因此她必須儘快採取行動，要愈快愈好。飯後，她邀請 James 去逛一個日夜都開門的大購貨中心，玩得很愉快。臨分手前，她又邀請他在次日晚間去她家吃飯，佯稱那天是她的生日。泰林高興地接受了邀請。他問她是否和她的父母一同住，她回答她和她的父母不住在一起，她一個人單獨住在一棟很小的公寓裡。

The more she thought about it, the more excited she became. But the American man said his vacation in China had only five days left, so she must take action as fast as possible. After the meal, she invited James to visit a large shopping mall which was open 24 hours, and they had a good time over there. Before saying good-bye, she further invited him to have dinner at her home the next evening, pretending that the next day was her birthday. Tai-lin happily accepted the invitation. When he asked her if she lived with her parents, she replied that she and her parents lived separately. She lived by herself at a small apartment.

第十一章　Chapter Eleven

蘋蘋要泰林六時半來，他帶了一束鮮花於六時二十九分鐘到達了她的住處。蘋蘋來開門，泰林做夢也想不到她竟然穿著幾乎是半透明的性感服裝來接待他。薄薄的粉紅色絲質襯衫，只有三四個釦子是釦著的，裡面似乎沒有戴奶罩，那兩隻動盪的豐碩乳房於走路時都可以隱隱看到。

Holding a bundle of flowers, Tai-lin reached Pin-pin's residence one minute before six-thirty, the time she told him to come. Pin-pin answered the door. Tai-lin was surprised to see her wearing an alluring dress to treat him. Putting on a thin pink silk shirt with only three or four buttons on and seemingly without wearing a bra, her two plum breasts bounced and could be partially seen when she walked.

泰林認識蘋蘋好多年了，可他從來沒有見過她除了臉和手臂外如此大膽地將她的身體顯露給一個男子看，而他現在還是一個認識不過一天的外國人。泰林曾經和天堂裡的仙女織成相處過一些時間，和陰間的鬼女友馨蒂同居了好幾個月，與美國護士 Donna 結婚半年多，他知道當一個女人如此打扮時她想要什麼。

Tai-lin had known Pin-pin for years, but he had never seen her so boldly showing her body other than her face and arms to a man, and he was now a foreigner who had known her for only one day. Tai-lin had stayed with Ze-chen, the fairy in Heaven, for a while, and had lived with Xin-di, his female ghost lover in the ghost world for many months, and he had married Donna, an American nurse for more than half a year. He knew what a woman wanted when she dressed like this.

用餐時，蘋蘋喝了很多杯葡萄酒，泰林記憶中她可是從來不喝酒的。而且她還不停地鼓勵他也喝。飯後，當他們在看電視時，她更情意綿綿地坐到他的懷中並且主動地親吻他。這個親密的舉動使得他想起了仙女織成，那個他第一次與之發生性關係的女人，情況非常類似。抱著這麼一個半裸的年輕美麗女子特別又是他的第一個戀人在懷中，他不能控制自己了，他也去吻她，並把一隻手伸進她那半開著的絲質襯衫裡去撫摸她的豐碩雙乳。終於，他們脫光了衣服，抱著在床上翻滾，最後做愛了。泰林發現這還是蘋蘋的初夜，他是她的第一個男人。

During the meal, Pin-pin drank several glasses of wine, which she had never done before as far as Tai-lin remembered. And she kept encouraging him to drink. After the meal, when they were watching television, she impulsively sat on his lap and kissed him. The intimate action reminded Tai-lin of the fairy Ze-chen with whom he had had his first sexual experience. This situation looked very familiar. With such a half-naked pretty young woman, especially his first lover, in his arms, he could not control himself. He kissed her back and extended a hand to go inside of her half opened silk shirt caressing her plump breasts. Finally, they rolled on the bed, totally naked, and made love. Tai-lin found it was still Pin-pin's first time, and he was her first man.

也許這是我應該得到的，應該在數年前就得到的。一句中國老話說，是你的不管發生什麼情況還是你的。不論我們之間發生了什麼事情，我仍是她命中註定的第一個男人，泰

林想著。

Maybe I deserved it and should have had it several years ago. An old Chinese old saying says, "If it belongs to you, it would come to you no matter what." I was destined to be her first man no matter what happened between us. Tai-lin thought.

當泰林回到他的旅館時，已經是下半夜了。他無法入眠，不是因為終於和蘋蘋做愛而太興奮了，而是因為她要求他為她做的事情。當他在床上撫摸她的身體時，她請求他娶她帶她去美國。那不正是她多年的夢想麼。如今泰林有這個能力去幫助她實現她的願望了，*我是否應當去做呢？我應當告訴她我是誰嗎？*

When Tai-lin returned to his hotel, it was after midnight. He could not sleep at all, not because he was too excited for having finally made love to Pin-pin, but because of what she had asked him to do for her. While caressing her on the bed, she asked him to marry her and take her to the United States. That was exactly what she had been dreaming of. Now Tai-lin had the ability to help her achieve her dream. *Should I go ahead and do it? Should I tell her who I am?*

他曾經為她而死，因為他不讚同她非法潛入美國的計劃，可是她似乎並不在乎他的死亡。他曾經想在柔和的月光下去擁抱她一下，可是她拒絕了。但是，她卻把她的初夜送給了一個完全不認識的美國男子，就因為這個外國人可以帶她去美國。突然，泰林感覺到非常不愉快，他為蘋蘋的行為羞恥。他愈想也就愈不愉快，也就愈為蘋蘋的行為感到無比的不齒。

He had died for her because he did not approve her illegal plan to smuggle herself into America, but she seemed not to care about his death. He had tried to hug her under the soft moonlight one evening, but she refused. And now she voluntarily gave her virginity to a totally unknown American man, just because the foreign man could take her to the United States. Suddenly, Tai-lin felt very much unhappy and was ashamed of Pin-pin's action. And the more he thought, the unhappier he became, and the more shameful he would feel for Pin-pin's behavior.

"這真是羞恥，一個絕大的羞恥！"他大聲地叫著。

"It was a shame, a great shame!" He yelled loudly.

但是，轉而一想，假如我把她帶去了美國，她到達了以後，她會快樂嗎？我住在新大陸已經好幾年了，在法理上，我是一個美國人，可是，在我的內心深處，我還是認為我是一個中國人。蘋蘋是個道地的中國女子，沒有受過很多正式的學校教育，去美國不過是她的夢想，一個不切實際的夢想。為了達到她的夢想，她做了昨天夜裡的事情。

But on second thought, if I take her to the United States anyway, will she be happy after she reaches there? I have lived in the new land for several years and legally I'm an American, but deep in my heart, I still consider myself a Chinese. Pin-pin is a typical Chinese woman, without much formal school education. Wishing to go to the United States is but her dream, an impractical dream. In order to fulfill her dream, she did what she had done last night.

在以往的相愛歲月中，她從來沒有讓我吻她，或甚至於擁抱一下。她是這麼一個保守的女性，那也是爲什麼我深深地愛著她的原因之一。現在，她主動將自己奉送給一個外國男子，就因爲這個外國人能使她的夢想成真。

During the years we loved each other, she never let me kiss her, or even hug her. She was such a conservative woman and that was one of the reasons why I loved her desperately. Now she was willing to offer herself to a foreign man just because the foreigner could make her dream materialize.

也許蘋蘋並不是唯一有這種夢的人，因爲很多其他的中國年輕女子都有這個夢。事實上，很多年輕的中國男子也有這個同樣的夢。如果中國像美國一樣地富裕，是否中國人民還會懷有這個夢？如果美國像現在的中國一樣，而中國又像現在的美國一樣，是不是所有的美國年輕人都夢想去中國？

Maybe Pin-pin was not the only one to have such a dream, as many other Chinese young women are dreaming the same dream. As a matter of fact, many Chinese young men are having

the same dream, too. If China were as rich as the United States,
would the Chinese still have this dream? And if the United
States were like the present China and China were like the
present United States, would all the American young people
dream of going to China?

人的夢想究竟是什麼，是追求物質上的享受還是精神上
的享受？那種比較長久？那種是永恆的？是不是根本沒有什
麼東西叫做永恆的？

What are the people dreaming of, physical pleasure or
spiritual pleasure? Which one will last longer? Which one will
be permanent? Or is there simply no such thing called
permanent?

因為對於這些問題找不到任何答案，他無法成眠，而坐
在那裡一直思索著這些問題。等他終於上床睡覺時，已經是
第二天的早晨了。

As he did not get the answers for the questions he raised,
he could not sleep but sat in meditation of those questions.
When he finally went to bed it was early morning of next day.

醒來後，他決定不再與蘋蘋見面，因為他仍然認為她前
天夜晚所做的是件羞恥的事情。雖然他已經佔有了她，他認
為是不公平的，前天夜晚佔有她的是 James，而那個為她死
亡的人是泰林。他是泰林，不是 James。泰林不欠她什麼，

可她欠泰林的太多了。讓泰林去完成她的夢想是不公平的。

After waking, he decided not to meet Pin-pin again, as he still considered shameful for what she had done the night before. Although he had claimed her, he thought it was unfair, because the man who had had her last night was James and the man who had died for her was Tai-lin. He was Tai-lin, not James. Tai-lin did not owe her anything, but she owed Tai-lin a lot. It was unfair for Tai-lin to help her fulfill her dream.

這是不公平的，對我來說是太不公平的！
It is unfair, totally unfair for me!

他不再繼續去思索，向旅館退了房，叫了部計程車直衝飛機場，他飛回了美國。

Without thinking any longer, he checked out of the hotel, called a taxi and rushed to the airport. He flew back to the United States.

他告訴自己，他必須忘記這個中國女人，這個他曾經深愛過多年的女人。他不再是他的愛人了，她不配做他的愛人。也許，沒有一個女人是他的愛人。他曾經愛過一位仙女，愛過一個女鬼，愛過一個美國女護士，如今這些都是過去的了。他不再對任何女人有興趣了，不管在中國還是美國，在天堂，在陰間，還是在人間。

He told himself he must forget the Chinese woman whom

he had loved so deeply for so many years in the past. She was not his lover anymore. She did not deserve to be his lover. Maybe no woman was his lover. He had once loved a fairy, a female ghost, and a female American nurse, and those were all in the past. He now was not interested in any woman, no matter where, China or America, Heaven or in the world of ghost, or in the world of humans.

第十二章　Chapter Twelve

　　和 James 一樣，泰林對建築事業沒有興趣。三個月後，他辭去家庭建築公司中的職務。不久，他在美國移民局丹佛分局裡找到了一份工作。在那裡他有很多的機會會見從世界各地特別是東南亞來的移民，他也處理來自這些地區的非法移民案件。

Like James, Tai-lin was not interested in the construction business. Three months later, he quit his job with his family's home-building company, and soon after obtained a position at the US Immigration and Naturalization Office in Denver. There he had many chances to meet immigrants from all over the world, especially the ones from southeastern Asia, and he often handled the cases of illegal aliens from those areas.

　　一天，他被指派處理一些來自中國的非法移民。當他發現蘋蘋的名字在這份名單中時，他大為震驚。

One day, he was assigned to a case involving some illegal aliens from China. When he learned that Pin-pin's name was on the list, he was shocked.

<u>林蘋蘋是一個非法移民，在丹佛的一家中國飯店裡打工！</u>他跳了起來，簡直不能相信他所看到的檔案。

<u>Pin-pin Lin is an illegal alien, working at a Chinese restaurant in Denver!</u> He jumped up, as he could not believe the document he had just read.

那更壞的事情是蘋蘋已經懷孕了差不多十個月，當她被捕時，她的健康情況非常惡劣。根據移民法規定，她應該被驅逐出境回到她原來的國家。可是，她的重病使得她不能搭乘那十三個鐘頭的飛回中國長途飛行。

And the worse thing was that Pin-pin had been pregnant for about ten months, and her health was in critical condition when she was arrested. According to the immigration laws, she should be deported back to the nation she came from. But she was very sick, unable to take the 13-hour return flight to China.

*十個月身孕？*他從中國回到美國已經十個月了。十個月前，他曾經在中國成都和蘋蘋做愛。現在，她懷孕了隨時可能生產。

Pregnant for ten months? He had returned to the United States from China for ten months. Ten months ago, he made love to Pin-pin in Chen-Du, China. Now she was pregnant and could give birth at any time.

她的嬰兒是我的嗎？假如是的，那這真是太巧合了！一個多麼殘酷的巧合！泰林不停地想著和喃喃自語。轉而一想，也許這個名叫林蘋蘋的非法女移民不是我以前的那個戀人，而是另一個同名同姓的中國女人？

Did I father her baby? If I did, what kind of coincidence it would be! And what kind of cruel coincidence it is! Tai-lin kept thinking and murmuring to himself. But on a second thought, *maybe the illegal woman named Pin-pin Lin is not the one I loved before but another Chinese woman with the same name?*

於是，他去拘留非法移民的處所察看。他看到了一個年輕懷孕的東方女子，她躺在床上閉著雙眼，似乎是病得不輕。"她是我的蘋蘋，不管她是如何地改變！"泰林迅即自語道。他回到了辦公室，突然間，他感到頭痛欲烈，就好像是被人用棍擊中一樣。他向上級請假一日，在家思索如何是好。結果，他一籌莫展。

So, he visited the place where the illegal aliens were detained. He saw a young pregnant Oriental woman lying on a bed with both eyes closed, seemingly very sick. She is my Pin-pin, no matter how much she had changed! Tai-lin said to himself right away, then, he retreated to his office. Suddenly, he came down with a severe headache as if somebody had used a cudgel to hit his head. He asked for the rest of day off. He stayed at home, trying to think of a way out of the predicament but failed completely.

第十三章　Chapter Thirteen

於是，泰林再度去拜訪蘋蘋。這次他安排與她在一間小屋子裡單獨見面。把門關上並鎖好了後，他用中文告訴她他是誰，及他又如何變成了個美國人。他不是美國人，他是她以前的愛人蔡泰林。他向她承認是他在十個月前和她在中國做愛，他是她肚子裡的孩子的父親，他要對她及他們的嬰兒負起一切的責任。

So, Tai-lin visited Pin-pin again. This time he arranged to meet her separately at a small room. After the door was closed and locked, he told her in Chinese who he was, and how he had become an American man. He was not American. He was her former lover, Tai-lin Cai. He also confessed to her that it was he who made love to her in China ten months ago. It was he who fathered her unborn baby. He told her he wanted to be responsible for her and their baby.

剛開始，蘋蘋嚇壞了，她不能相信他的故事。但是，當她認出了他的中國口音及他敘述他們的愛情是那麼地真而又確時，她終於接受了這個世界上最難使人相信的故事。他們擁抱，他們接吻，他們又悲又喜地叫喊著。

In the beginning, Pin-pin was baffled, finding his story hard to believe. But when she recognized his Chinese voice, and his descriptions of their love story in China were not only details but also true, she finally accepted the most unbelievable tale in the world. They hugged, kissed, and bitterly and joyfully cried.

泰林答允蘋蘋，"首先，我將安排你去醫院，等孩子生下後，我就和你結婚，你和我們的孩子就可以合法而又快樂地和我永遠永遠住在美國。"

Tai-lin promised Pin-pin, "First of all, I'm going to make an arrangement to send you to a hospital. After you give birth, I'll marry you, and you and our baby will be able to stay in the United States with me legally and happily forever and forever."

"啊，泰林，"蘋蘋興奮地問道，"我是不是在夢中？"

"Oh, Tai-lin," Pin-pin was excited and asked him, "Am I in a dream?"

"不，這是真的！我們兩人都在美國，這不就是你以前的夢想麼？你的夢想現在成真了。"

"No, it is real! We are both in the United States. This is what you dreamed before. Your dream has now materialized."

蘋蘋感受太深了，她一句話再也說不出來，讓泰林靜靜地擁抱著她，讓快樂的眼淚順著雙頰流過不停。

Pin-pin was so moved that she could not say a word more but let Tai-lin hold her, and let her tears of happiness flow freely down her cheeks.

悲傷的是當蘋蘋到達醫院時，她的健康狀況已經迅速惡化。

Sadly, Pin-pin's health rapidly deteriorated when she arrived at the hospital.

也許老天爺故意為難，指定照顧蘋蘋的護士竟是 Donna Jones，泰林的前妻。泰林很尷尬，可是 Donna 很鎮靜，她很有興趣要查出她的前夫與這個從中國來的生病非法女移民的關係。

Maybe Heaven interfered purposely. The nurse who was assigned to take care of Pin-pin was Donna Jones, Tai-pin's ex-wife. Tai-lin was embarrassed, but Donna was calm, and she was very interested in finding out the relationship between her former husband and the sick female illegal alien from China.

在這種情況下，泰林選擇了誠實，他把整個的實在情形一五一十地告訴了 Donna。Donna 終於相信了她的前夫根本就從來沒有過任何精神疾病。當她在丹佛 First Denver Memorial Hospital 第一次見到他時，那時他被診斷為一個精神病人，那個時候她就很懷疑他是否真的有病。如今，在這整個的世界上，Donna 是唯一真正瞭解泰林的人了。

Under such circumstances, Tai-lin chose honesty. He told Donna the whole truth. Donna finally believed that her ex-husband had never had a mental problem. When she fist met him at the First Denver Memorial Hospital while Tai-lin was diagnosed as a psychiatric patient, she was somewhat doubtful of his sickness. Now in the whole world, she became the only person who understood Tai-lin completely.

Donna 答應泰林她定會給予蘋蘋最好的照顧。

Donna promised Tai-lin she would give Pin-pin the best care she could.

雖然如此，蘋蘋在生產時還是死亡了。

Nevertheless, Pin-pin still died in giving birth to her baby.

泰林傷心欲絕，旋又興奮地發現嬰兒存活了。小嬰兒是個女孩。Donna 把小嬰兒抱在懷裡，她安慰泰林並向他保證她會幫助他照顧他的女兒的。泰林很感動，向她深致謝忱。

Tai-lin was heartbroken, but soon he was thrilled as the baby survived. The baby was a girl. Holding the infant in her arms, Donna comforted Tai-lin and assured him that she would help him take care of his daughter. Tai-lin was deeply moved and appreciative of her kindness.

現在，Donna 是全世界上唯一瞭解及相信他的故事的人了，當然，那最重要的因素是因為他們兩人仍然深愛著對方，所以在把蘋蘋的遺體火化了一個月後，泰林和 Donna 兩人又結婚了，婚後 Donna 又將泰林的女兒正式辦理了收養手續。他們為他們的小女兒起名憶蘋，中文的意思表示懷念蘋蘋。

Since Donna was now the only person in the whole world who knew and believed his story, and of course, the most important thing was that they still loved each other, one month after cremating Pin-pin's remains, Tai-lin and Pin-pin remarried. Donna adopted Tai-lin's baby daughter after marriage. They named their daughter Yi-pin. Literally in Chinese it meant remembering of Pin-pin.

第十四章　Chapter Fourteen

帶著蘋蘋的一個小骨灰盒子，泰林飛去中國。他在蘋蘋死亡前曾經答應過她，他會親自把她的骨灰盒子送給她的父母親的。

Carrying the small box with Pin-pin's ashes in it, Tai-lin flew to China. He had promised Pin-pin before she died that he would personally take her ashes to her parents.

在這十三個鐘頭的長途飛行中，泰林一直不停地思索著他與蘋蘋的既甜又苦的愛情。*假如當初康復成衣工廠從不曾決定要把他們的產品銷售到海外市場去，他們就不會成立一*

個外銷部，而研讀英文也就不會在工廠裡如此盛行，那麼，蘋蘋也就不會決心去讀英文和想去美國，而她和我就會早已愉快地結婚了；當然，我也就不會自殺而她也不會死在美國了。

During the 13-hour flight, Tai-lin kept thinking about his bitter and sweet love with Pin-pin. *If Comfort Garment Factory had never decided to extend their sales to the overseas market, they would not have created an export department and studying English would not have become popular in the factory. Then Pin-pin would not have been so determined to study English and wish to go to the United States, and she and I would probably have been happily married, and of course, I would not have committed suicide, and she would not have died in America.*

多年來，她一直夢想去美國，她終於成功了，可她萬萬沒有想到她會死在這新大陸。假如我不曾回去中國，我就不會有機會遇到她還和她做愛，那麼，她就不會懷孕。假如她不曾懷孕，她就不會死亡。如此推論，我是個兇手，我是'殺死'她的兇手，這就如同當初她'殺死'了我。這兩個悲慘事件如此出人意料地發生了，沒有人想要這麼做而事情竟然發生了；人的一生真是多麼無法預料！

She had dreamed of going to the United States for years and had finally made it, but she never expected that her life would end in the new land. If I had not returned to China, I would not have had a chance to meet her again and made love to her, and she would not have become pregnant. If she had not been pregnant, she would not have died. In this case, I'm the murderer. I "killed" her just like she had "killed" me before. The two sad things happened so unexpectedly. Nobody really wanted to do these things and things had happened. A human being's life is indeed totally unpredictable!

泰林找到了蘋蘋的父母親，把蘋蘋的骨灰盒子交給了他們。他沒有告訴這對老夫婦他是誰，只說他是蘋蘋在美國的美國男朋友。臨走時，他留給這對老人一萬元美金，告訴他們那是他們女兒的錢。事實上，只有不到四分之一的錢是蘋蘋在死亡前留下給他的。

Tai-lin found Pin-pin's parents and delivered the box of Pin-pin's bone ashes to them. He did not tell the senior couple who he was, but said that he was Pin-pin's American boyfriend in the United States. Before leaving, he left the couple ten thousand US dollars, telling them it was their daughter's money. Actually, only less than one fourth was what Pin-pin had left to him before her death.

現在，他完成了他爲蘋蘋所做的最後一件他認爲他應該做的事情了，突然間，他感覺輕鬆多了。

Now he had done the last thing for Pin-pin as he thought he had the obligation to do. Suddenly, he felt much relieved.

　　既然蘋蘋已經死亡，泰林知道他今後可能不再有機會來成都了。不知道為什麼，他突然決定在返回美國前再上一次峨嵋山，在那裡，他開始他那顛簸複雜的一生，他遇見仙女織成，她帶他去了一趟天堂。

　　Since Pin-pin had died, Tai-lin knew that probably he would not have a chance to visit Chen-du again in the future. Without knowing why, he suddenly decided to go one more time to the E-Mei Mountain before returning to the United States as his complicated fate began there when he met Ze-chen, the fairy, who took him to Heaven.

第十五章　Chapter Fifteen

　　泰林上了山。他到達他當年在那裡就如何處理與蘋蘋的關係而沉思的地方，在那裡，他完全意外地遇見了織成，她把他帶上了天堂。現在，他孤獨地逗留在那兒沒有發現任何其他人。美麗的山景似乎沒有任何變化，藍色的晴空依然可愛。三年了，一切沒有改變；可是，他卻從一個中國工廠工人變成一個美國移民局的官員。他曾經去過天堂，也去過陰間，最後，他又回到了人間，現在住在美國。除了他的中國愛人蘋蘋，他曾經和一個仙女織成做過愛，他曾經愛過一個女鬼馨蒂，一個美國女護士 Donna Jones，他還和這個女護士結了婚，後來又離婚，現在又再度結婚。他分析比較他生命中的這四個女人。

　　Tai-lin went up the mountain. He reached the place where

he had meditated about what to do with Pin-pin. It was there he unexpectedly met Ze-chen who took him to Heaven. He stayed at the spot all by himself, as he had found nobody else in sight. The beautiful mountain views seemed to be the same and the blue sky was lovely as well. Nothing had changed during the past three years, but he had changed from a Chinese factory worker to an American immigration official. He had been to Heaven and the world of ghosts, and later he had returned to the world of humans and now he lived in the United States. Besides his Chinese lover, Pin-pin, he had made love with a fairy, Ze-chen, and he had loved a female ghost, Xin-di, and an American female nurse, Donna Jones, whom he married and divorced then remarried. He compared the four women in his life.

織成一天到晚無憂無慮，她和蘋蘋及 Donna 完全不同，也許她和馨蒂還有些類似，她們兩個都從不去憂愁，不論在何種情況下都能找尋快樂，唯一的不同那就是一個是仙女，一個是女鬼。

Ze-chen was carefree all the time. She was totally different from Pin-pin or Donna. Perhaps she might be somewhat similar to Xin-di. Neither of the two women worried. They knew how to find pleasure for themselves no matter in what situations. The only difference was that one was a fairy and the other one, a ghost.

也許這些都是她們的命運，被安排控制的命運。誰控制她們的命運呢？如果命運是註定的，命運也可以改變嗎？如果答案是可以，那又是如何去改變呢？

Maybe those are their fates, arranged and controlled by someone. Who is the one who controls the fates for them? If the fates are predestined, can they be changed? If the answer is yes, then how can they be changed?

突然，他希望能夠找到一個權威人士來和他談論這些問題。

Suddenly, he wished to find a person in such authority and discuss those questions with him.

第十六章　Chapter Sixteen

於回到居住的旅館途中，他碰巧在山腳下經過一座佛教廟宇。他曾經聽說過一個佛教有道高僧能夠回答這些他剛才想到的問題，於是，他走進了廟宇，順便想休息一下。

On the way back to hotel where he stayed, Tai-lin happened to pass by a Buddhist temple by the foot of mountain. He had heard that a knowledgeable Buddhist monk was often able to answer those types of questions he had just raised. So he walked into the temple to take a rest anyway.

從建築上看來，這座廟宇已經很老了，可是它一定在最

近整修過了，因爲大殿牆上的油漆看起來還很新。除了大雄
寶殿外，兩邊還有很多較小的房間。泰林沒有發現一個和尙，
但是，他看到很多穿著海青的尼姑往來於大殿及其他的房
間。泰林疑慮是否還要找個尼姑來和他談論這些困擾的難
題，於是他坐在前院中的一張木頭座位上就這個問題再作思
考。

From the construction, it seemed that it was a very old
temple, but it must have been remodeled not too long ago, as
the paint on the walls was still fresh and new. Besides the main
hall, there were many smaller rooms at both sides. Tai-lin did
not meet any monks, but he saw many nuns in Buddhist
uniforms going in and out between the main hall and the other
rooms. Tai-lin wondered if he still wanted to find a nun to
discuss those perplexities with her. He sat on a wooden seat in
the front yard thinking about this question.

就在這個時候，他突然看見一個熟悉的美麗女子，不，
是個年輕的女尼，經過他的身邊。他立刻站起加快腳步跟了
上去，於是，他萬分驚訝地發現這個年輕美麗的女尼長得很
像織成，那個三年前曾經把他帶上天堂一遊的仙女。他乃不
加思索地用中文高聲叫著織成的名字，來試試這個尼姑答應
與否。如果她答應了，那她就真的可能是這個仙女；如果不
答應，那就不是織成。

Just at this moment, he glanced toward a familiar pretty
woman, no, a young nun, passing by him. He quickly stood up

and hastened his steps trying to follow her. And he was shocked to discover that the pretty young nun looked very much like Ze-chen, the fairy who took him to Heaven three years ago. Without too much hesitation, he loudly called Ze-chen's name in Chinese to see if the nun would answer or not. If she answered, she might truly be the fairy. If not, she would not be Ze-chen.

*這很可能的，當我心裡想著織成時，我就會把任何一個美麗年輕女子當作她了，*他想。

It is very possible, when I thought of Ze-chen in mind, I would misjudge any pretty young woman as her, he thought.

非常奇怪地，這個女尼停下了腳步並回轉頭來向他望去。她萬分驚訝地問泰林剛才說什麼。泰林突然想起了他現在已經不像個中國人而是個外國人了，他在想如何回答女尼的問話。

Surprisingly, the nun stopped and turned her head toward him. She asked in amazement what Tai-lin had just said. Tai-lin suddenly remembered that he now was not in appearance like a Chinese but a foreigner. So he was figuring how to answer the nun's question.

在泰林還未再度開口說話前，女尼又問他如何知道她以前的名字。（當一個人變成為和尚或尼姑後，這個人將會有一個佛教的法號,而不再用他或她原來的名字了。)泰林立刻用流利的中國話告訴她他的中國名字,及簡單地解釋他如何變成了一個美國人。

Before Tai-lin said any more words, the nun asked him again how he had learned her old name. (When a person became a Buddhist monk or nun, the person must take a Buddhist name, and not to use his or her original name anymore.) Tai-lin quickly told her his Chinese name in fluent Chinese language, and briefly explained how he had become an American man.

聽完了泰林的故事後,她要他跟著她走到附近的一間小空房間。在那裡她向她承認她就是織成,從天堂裡來的仙女。於是,他們相互告訴對方自從三年前她把他帶回地面上後所發生的一切情形。

After hearing Tai-lin's story, she asked him to follow her into a nearby small empty room. There she admitted to him that she was truly Ze-chen, the fairly from Heaven. Then they started to tell each other about what had happened since she took him down to the earth three years ago.

根據織成所說,那天她把泰林送去人間回到天堂後,她就接到了天堂主宰者辦公室的一張通知,要她去談話。她立刻去了。天堂主宰者告訴她他收到了另一個仙女的報告,聲稱她曾經幫助一個凡人混進天堂,南天門前兩隻負責守衛的白色老虎也證實了織成的不法行為。織成想起來了,那天在舞廳裡當另一個名叫麗麗的仙女和泰林跳舞時，她曾經問過他幾個問題，因爲泰林沒有回答她關於他背景的問題，她懷疑泰林在天堂裡的身份。這個心胸狹窄仙女就向天堂主宰者報告織成沒有經過核准非法將一個凡人帶進了天堂。

According to Ze-chen, soon after she returned Heaven from taking Tai-lin down to the world of humans, she received a notice from the office of the grand ruler in Heaven asking her to come to his office. She did immediately. The ruler told her that he had received a report from another fairy saying that she had helped a mortal sneak into Heaven, and the two white tigers guarding the Southern Heaven Gate also witnessed Ze-chen's illegal action. Ze-chen remembered that when Li-li, another fairy, danced with Tai-lin in the dancing hall, she asked him a few questions. Because Tai-lin did not answer her inquiry about his background, she suspected Tai-lin's status in Heaven. The narrow-minded fairy reported to the Heavenly ruler about Ze-chen's illegal activities of bringing a mortal into Heaven without approval in advance.

根據天堂的律法，織成被處罰去人間三年接受人間的苦難，在這段期間內，她的超自然神功被暫停了。織成不想混在一般人民中間，她變成了一個尼姑。她的三年處罰期將於次日完畢，然後她就會重新獲得她的超自然神功而飛回天堂。真是好奇怪啊，她在處罰期完畢變回爲仙女的前夕又能遇到這個使她違犯天規的男子。泰林和織成對於他們的重逢真有說不出來的興奮。

Based on the rules in Heaven, Ze-xhen was punished to stay in the world of humans to suffer as a mortal for three years. During this period, her supernatural powers were suspended. As Ze-chen did not want to mingle with the common people, she became a Buddhist nun. Her three years of punishment was going to expire the next day, then, she would reclaim her supernatural power and fly back to Heaven. How strange it was for her to have a chance to meet Tai-lin, the person who made her break the Heavenly rules, before she turned back into a fairy! Naturally, both Tai-lin and Ze-chen were excited about their reunion.

　　當他們在興高采烈地相互敘述自己的故事時，廟宇裡的大鐘高聲地響了起來。織成告訴泰林，這是要所有的尼姑們都到大殿裡去在方丈的監督下研讀佛經，她說她必須服從廟宇的規律因為她目前還是個尼姑。然後，她站起身來很不願意地向泰林說再見，同時真誠地祝福他在美國與 Donna 的婚姻愉快。當她走了幾步後，又回轉頭來向著泰林微微一笑。泰林記得那個笑容，世界上最迷人的微笑沒有一點兒的人工成分，織成永遠是年輕美麗的，從來沒有變老。

When they were joyfully telling each other's stories as much details as they could remember, they were distracted by the loud ringing of the temple's bell. Ze-chen told Tai-lin that it was the time for all the nuns to go to the main hall to study the

Buddhist classics under the strict supervision of their chief priest. She said she had to follow the rules while she was still a nun. Then she reluctantly said good-bye to Tai-lin and sincerely wished him a happy married life with Donna in the United States. Reluctantly, she stood up and left for the main hall. After a few steps, she turned her head toward Tai-lin and gave him a smile. Tai-lin remembered that smile, the most bewitching smile without any human's make up. Ze-chen was always young and pretty, never grew older.

泰林一個人坐在這個房間裡沉思，一直到黑暗籠罩著大地，然後他離開了廟宇。第二天，他飛回了美國。

Tai-lin sat alone in the room in meditation until darkness covered the world, then, he left the temple. The next day, he flew back to the United States.

回到美國的家中後，他告訴 Donna 如何意想不到地和織成重逢的經過，Donna 很驚訝。接著她對他說，"我告訴你一件事情，你可能也覺得驚訝。"

After reaching home, he told Donna about his unexpected reunion with Ze-chen. Donna was surprised. Then, she said to him, "I would tell you something which might surprise you, too."

Donna 說自從她照顧她們的女兒憶蘋後，她就從來沒有發現這個嬰兒啼哭，相反地，這個小女孩整天都呈現著快樂的樣子。"她長大後她一定會是個無憂無憂的樂天派女子，" Donna 愉快地說。

Donna said that ever since she began to take care of their baby daughter, Yi-pin, she had found the baby never cried. Instead, the little girl looked happy all the time. "She will become a carefree woman when she grows up," Donna said happily.

*一個無憂無憂的樂天派女子？*泰林突然想起了另一個無憂無憂的樂天派女子，他的陰間女友，馨蒂。他迅速將嬰兒從 Donna 手中接了過來抱在懷中。對著他的女兒凝視了一分鐘，然後突然感到非常震驚，他興奮地告訴他的妻子，

"Donna，我相信我們的女兒是我的陰間鬼女友投胎的，不僅她的無憂無憂的樂天派性格像馨蒂，就是她的五官也很像她。"

A carefree woman? Tai-lin suddenly thought of another carefree young woman, his ghost girlfriend, Xin-di. He quickly took the baby from Donna's hands and held her in his arms. Staring at his daughter in bewilderment, he told his wife excitedly, "Donna, I would believe our daughter is my ghost girlfriend, Xin-di, to be reborn. Not only her carefree character resembles Xin-di, but so do her features."

接著他告訴 Donna，馨蒂一定是在等候他從陽世歸來可

一直沒有他的消息，因此對他非常失望。當她投胎轉世的時刻到了的時候，她可能要求閻羅王讓她投生爲泰林和蘋蘋的女兒。如果這是真的，那麼，這種命運的安排對她和他真是太有意義了！也真的太公平了！

Then, he told Donna that Xin-di must have waited for his return from the trip of the human world for too long and become disappointed. When her time to be reborn as a human again came, she might ask the ghost ruler to let her be born as Tai-lin and Pin-pin's daughter. If that was the case, how horrible the fate had been arranged for her and him! And how fair it was!

泰林一手抱著他的女兒，另一隻手緊緊地摟著他的妻子Donna，他們並坐在一張情人椅上，很久很久說不出一句話來。

Tai-lin cradled his daughter in one hand and used the other one to hug his wife, Donna, tightly. They sat on a love seat without saying a word for a long, long time.

每一個人都有夢想。蘋蘋夢想去美國，她終於達成了她的夢想，可是她在新大陸並不如她預期的快樂，後來更意想不到地死在這裡。

Everybody has a dream. Pin-pin dreamed of going to the United States, and she eventually made it but she was not as happy as expected and died in the new land.

　　我夢想和她結婚，在中國有一個快樂的婚姻生活。結果我沒有得到，後來竟驚奇地在美國愉快地也許是悲痛地和她重逢，可這個重逢並沒有維持多久。

　　I dreamed of marrying her, having a happy married life in China, but I did not have it, then, surprisingly we had a happy, maybe sad, reunion in the United States, but the reunion did not last very long.

　　織成夢想永遠生活在天堂裡，可是她觸犯了天律，被罰下凡塵三年，遭受她從來沒有遭遇過的苦痛。

　　Ze-chen dreamed of living in Heaven forever, but she broke the Heavenly laws and was published to stay in the world of humans for three years suffering what she had never had.

　　馨蒂夢想和我在陰間一起度過最後的兩年半，可她沒有見到我回來，相反地，她竟變成了我在美國的女兒。

　　Xin-di dreamed of having her last two and half years with me in the world of ghosts. She did not see me back. Instead, she became my daughter in the United States.

　　Donna 夢想和我有一個幸福的婚姻，第一次她沒有得到，真想不到我們竟然愉快地又結婚了。

　　Donna dreamed of having a happy marriage with me originally, but she did not have it in her first try, and unexpectedly we happily remarried.

每個人都很努力希望他或她的夢想成真。夢想在沒有實現以前，應該是世界上最美麗的事情之一，所以人們不斷地有夢想；當他們的夢想破滅了，他們又變成失望了。

Everybody worked hard trying to make his or her dream materialized. A dream is supposed to be one of the most beautiful things in the world before it becomes true. So people keep having dreams and people keep becoming disappointed when their dreams are not fulfilled as they hoped.

泰林吻著他的妻子，又吻他的女兒。他告訴 Donna 他剛才所想到的一切，問她她的新夢想是什麼。Donna 回吻了她的丈夫，告訴他，她只夢想和他永遠永遠在一起，看到他們的女兒成長爲一個幸福的女人。

Tai-lin kissed his wife, then his daughter. He told Donna what he had just thought and asked her what her new dream was. Donna kissed him back, telling him that she just dreamed of being with him forever and forever and seeing their daughter grow into a gorgeous woman.

於是這對夫婦把他們的女兒放進搖籃裡，兩個人緊緊地擁抱，讓快樂的淚水沿著他們的雙頰流個下停。

Then, the couple put their daughter in her crib and hugged tightly with tears of joy running down freely on their cheeks.

（故事完畢）

（End of the Story）

作者的筆記 Author's Notes

五年前，因爲商業上的關係，我去了一次科羅拉多州的丹佛市。一天晚間，我在一家很小的中國飯店內吃飯，我的鄰桌坐著一對三十出頭的白人夫婦及一個小女孩，小女孩的頭髮是黑色的，還有一張東方人的面孔。最使我對這三個人有興趣的是當這個男子和他的中國女侍講話時，如果你不看他的面孔只聽他的說話，你可以肯定他是個來自中國的中國人。在我們的飯還未吃完前，我們就成爲了朋友，並交換了姓名。他告訴我他的名字是 James W.Cubin，婦人是他的妻子 Donna，小女孩是他們的女兒，憶蘋。

Five years ago, I made a business trip to Denver, Colorado. One evening, when I ate at a small Chinese restaurant, a couple of white people in early thirties, together with a little girl who had a black hair and an Oriental-looking face, sat at the table next to mine. What most interested me about the threesome was that when the man was speaking with his Chinese waitress, his Chinese language was so fluent that if you weren't looking at him you would swear he was a native Chinese from China. Before the end of our meals, we became friends and exchanged names. He told me his name was James W.Cubin and the woman was his wife, Donna. The little girl was their daughter, Yi-pin.

從此後 James 和我就經常通電話及電子信件，我們談論著中國歷史上及政治上的各種事件。每次我們都使用中文，很少用英文。似乎是 James 的英語和我一樣有著濃厚的外國腔調。我一直不明白這麼一個土生土長美國人的英語爲什麼也會有外國腔調，但我從來沒有當面問過他，只羨慕他對中國及中國文化風俗瞭解之深。

Since then, James and I had often exchanged phone calls and e-mails discussing many Chinese historical and political issues. Every time, we used Chinese, seldom in English. Seems to me James' English language was pretty much like mine, with a strong foreign accent. I always wondered how a native-born American's English could also have foreign accent, but I never asked him, only envied his rich knowledge about China and the Chinese culture and customs.

因爲我與丹佛有著商業上的聯繫，所以我幾乎每個月都要去一次這個中西部最大的城市。因爲 James 是我在這個區域中唯一會說流利中國話及能與之談論中國問題的朋友，每次在我公務辦完後，我就會電話他約他到中國飯店中去吃頓飯。偶而他也會邀請我去他家中用餐，他的妻子 Donna 的中美兩國菜都燒得很可口，雖然她不會說中國話，對我卻非常友善，他們的小女兒憶蘋長得可愛極了，整天無憂無慮的，我特別喜歡看她的笑容，那真是我多年來所見到過的最甜美的笑容。

Since I had some business connections in Denver, I visited

the largest city in the Midwest states just about every month. As James was my only friend in that area who could speak fluent Chinese to discuss the current Chinese issues with me, every time soon after I finished my business, I would call and invite him to have a supper at a Chinese restaurant. And occasionally, he invited me to eat at his house. His wife, Donna, was a good cook in both American and Chinese cuisines and she was very friendly to me although she did not speak Chinese. Their little daughter, Yi-pin, was very cute, carefree all the time. I particularly enjoyed her smile, the sweetest one I had seen in years.

五個月前，James 來到我和我的家人居住的休士頓。在電話中，他告訴我是來看他也住在休士頓的表哥的。在他拜訪他的表哥後，我請他在一家中國飯店中吃飯，飯後我把他帶回我的家中。到了我的家中後，他告訴我他實在是特別為我而來的，因為他要和我單獨作一長談。於是我們兩人坐在我的書房中，讓我的妻子耀文一個人在客廳裡看電視。

Five months ago, James came to Houston where I lived with my family. In the phone call, he told me he came to visit his cousin who also lived in Houston. Naturally, I invited him to eat at a Chinese restaurant after he had visited his cousin, then, I brought him home. In my home, he told me that the main reason for this trip was actually wishing to have a long private talk with me. So, we two sat in my study, while my wife,

Yaowen, was watching TV in our living room alone.

"Tom，" James 剛坐下，他就用流利的中國話問我，
"你可知道我是誰嗎？"

"Tom," James said in his fluent Chinese soon after he took
seat, "do you know who I'm?"

"你是 James W.Cubin。" 這真是一個非常簡單也可以
說是個愚笨的問題了，所以我毫不猶豫地回答。

"You're James W.Cubin." That was indeed a very simple,
maybe stupid, question, so I answered without any hesitation.

"不，我不是。和你一樣，我是一個中國人，我不是美
國人，而且 James W.Cubin 也不是我的名字。"

"No, I'm not. Like you, I'm a Chinese. I'm not American,
and James W.Cubin is not my name."

突然間，我驚駭不已。看起來他好像還沒有把要說的話
說完，我乃一言不發，審慎地聽下去。

Suddenly, I was taken aback. It seemed that he had not
finished what he wanted to tell me, so I said nothing, but
listened seriously.

"我原來是個名叫蔡泰林的中國鬼魂，我在 James
W.Cubin 於中國死亡後，借他的屍體還魂的。" 他站了起來，

以那我所見到過的最嚴肅的語態告訴我。

"Originally, I was a Chinese ghost named Tai-lin Cai. I revived as a human again on James W.Cubin's body after he had died in China." He stood up and told me in the most serious manner I had ever seen.

"我不相信，"我打斷他的話說道，"雖然我以前曾經讀過一些中國書上說，一個鬼魂可以借助一個剛死的人的屍體還魂過來，我非常相信這些都是道聽途說，完全沒有科學的憑證。"

"I don't believe it," I interrupted him, "Although I have read some Chinese books saying that a ghost can revive as a human again by a way of borrowing a newly dead person's body, I strongly believe that those are totally hearsay without any scientific proof."

"世界上幾乎每天都有很多不合乎科學的奇怪事情發生。你讀過佛教和基督教的經典嗎？這些書上也記載著很多使人難以相信的神怪事跡，可是人們都毫不懷疑地相信它們。"他坐了下來安靜地回答我。

"There are a lot of strange things happening about every day without scientists' agreement. Have you ever read the scriptures of Buddhism and Christianity? There are many unbelievable supernatural events in those books, but people believe them without any doubt," he sat down and answered me calmly.

　　在我又要說什麼前，他接著又說，「請耐心地聽我的故事。」

Before I was able to say something else, he added, "Please do have patience to listen to my story."

　　這上面的故事，「天堂遊」就是那天他告訴我的他的故事。

The above story, *A Visit to Heaven*, was what he had told me about himself that day.

　　至於他為什麼單獨挑選我來聽他的秘密，他說，「第一，你是我在美國的最好的朋友，你是個中國人，可是你歸化入美國籍已經好幾十年了。你說中國話及洞悉中國的歷史和在中國受過良好教育的中國人一樣，同時，你對美國的瞭解比我深廣多了。因此，我認為你最有資格聽我的故事。」

As for the reasons why he particularly chose me to listen to his secret, he said, "First, you're my best friend in the United States. You are a Chinese, but you have been naturalized as a US citizen for many decades. You speak the Chinese language and know the Chinese history as good as any educated Chinese in China. Meanwhile, your knowledge about the United States is much broader than mine. Therefore, I believe you're the most suitable person to listen to my story."

　　他喝了一口我奉上的一杯綠茶，又繼續說下去，"第二，也是最重要的理由，我知道你是個作家，一個中英文雙語作家，特別喜歡去寫神秘的故事。因此，我希望你能把我的故事寫下來作爲歷史的見證。"

He sipped the Chinese green tea I offered to him, then, continued, "Second, also the most important reason is that I know you're a writer, a Chinese and English bilingual writer, especially fond of writing the mysterious stories. Therefore, I would wish you could write my story for the world's record."

　　"但是，你的故事是很難使我的讀者們相信的，"我告訴他實話。

"But your story is so hard for my readers to believe," I told him, speaking the truthfully.

　　"那沒有關係，"他微笑著，然後又繼續解釋，"如果，也許我應當說當你的讀者們拒絕相信時，你不防告訴他們這是你自己的作品，一篇小說；因爲我知道你曾經是美國神秘小說作家協會裡的一個正級會員，同時你也是美國愛情小說作家協會和休士頓作家協會及休士頓華人作家協會的會員。你曾經把中國最神秘的小說集聊齋翻譯爲英文，將文稿賣給兩家美國出版公司，第一本包含二十三個故事由紐約的 Barricade Books 出版公司予以出版了，書名 Chinese Ghost Stories for Adults；第二本包含二十一個故事由伊黎諾州的 Help Publishing, Inc.出版公司予以出版了，書名 Tutor。後來，你又將這兩本英文書翻譯爲中文，交給中國兩家出版公司出版了漢英對照本。所以，非常可能地你的讀者們將會認爲我的一生不過是你寫的一個現代聊齋故事而已。如果真是這樣的話，對我來說是完全可以理解的。我不能強迫別人相信我的故事；事實上，有時候連我自己也不相信。

"That's all right," he smiled, then kept on explaining, "If, or I should say when your readers refuse to believe it, you may simply tell them this is but one of your own works, a fiction, as I know that you have been once an active member of the Mystery Writers of America besides Romance Writers of America and Houston Writers League as well as Houston Chinese Writers' Association. You have translated the most fantastic Chinese mystery book, *Liao Zhai*, into English and sold your manuscripts to two American publishers. The first one with 23 stories was published by Barricade Books in New York, titled *Chinese Ghost Stories for Adults,* and the second one with 21 stories was published by Helm Publishing, Inc. in Illinois, titled *Tutor.* You have also translated the two English books into Chinese and had two Chinese publishers in China publish them again bilingually in Chinese and English. So, it is very possible that your readers might take my story as another modern Liao Zhai tale. When that happens, it will be perfectly all right with me. I can not force people to believe my story, as sometimes I can not even believe it myself, too."

好了，我的親愛的讀者朋友們，你要我還能說什麼呢？相信這個故事與否是你的事情；對我來說，至少我已經完成了我的朋友 James W.Cubin 或者說蔡泰林要求我爲他所做的事情了。

Well, my dear readers, what else do you want me to say? Whether you believe this story or not, that's your business. At least, I have done my part as far as what my friend, James W.Cubin, or Tai-lin Cai, asked me to do.

多餘的後記

這篇小說早在多年前就寫好了，當初是用英文撰稿的。如果你問我從那裡來的靈感來寫這個荒謬不堪的怪異奇情現代聊齋故事，我的回答是這話還得從二十多年前說起。

一九八七年，那時我們全家住在美國懷俄明州一個名叫 Riverton 的城市。在一個偶然的機會裡，我接受了一個挑戰，替當地的唯一一份英文日報 The Ranger 撰寫每週專欄。內容和題目可以由我自行決定，不過應於每週二交稿，如此才可以於週四見報。

我們都知道每年十月底是美國的萬聖節，也就是俗稱的所謂鬼節。在這天裡，很多美國人特別是兒童們都喜歡穿著像妖魔鬼怪一樣的衣服，把面孔畫得怪模怪樣地裝成魔鬼的形象。爲了適應節日的氣氛，我就從"聊齋誌異"中選出一篇鬼怪故事將它改寫爲英文，作爲我那一週的專欄。我的本意不過是想告訴我的美國讀者們我們中國的女鬼是多麼地美麗和溫柔，不但不可怕，簡直是可愛極了。連續好幾年（我爲該報共寫了十四年的每週專欄），每年萬聖節時我都寫這麼一篇應景文章，每次都收到很多讀者們的熱烈反應，告訴我他們是多麼地盼望萬聖節能夠早日來臨。一些讀者們更建議我在不是萬聖節時不妨也寫些這類的中國神奇鬼怪故事。我乃與報紙總編輯 Dave Perry 商量，Dave 不太同意。他說這就好像不是萬聖節時我們沒有人去穿那些像魔鬼一樣的衣服。

　　於是有幾位讀者乃建議我索性去將這本中國鬼怪故事書多翻譯一些出版爲一本專書，相信在美國的書市上一定會有很好的銷路的。這就是我當初想翻譯“聊齋誌異”這本書爲英文的直接動機。

　　於是我將蒲松齡的這本曠世傑作再度重頭去讀，左選右選，選了二十三個故事將之改寫爲英文。由曾經出版過我一本英文散文集的紐約 Barricade Books 出版公司於西元兩千年予以出版了，書名就叫做 Chinese Ghost Stories for Adults。後來我將該書又自譯爲中文，並與上海世界圖書出版公司簽約出版漢英對照本，書名“聊齋精選”。這是 2005 年間的事了。

　　三年前我又從聊齋中選譯了另二十一個故事爲英文，並與美國伊黎諾州的 Helm Publishing Inc. 簽訂出版合同，該書於 2007 年 4 月問世，書名 Tutor。不久，Tutor 就被一個美國讀書人團體評爲 2007 年內一百本好書之一。我乃又將 Tutor 翻譯爲中文，並與中國安徽人民出版社簽訂出版合同，於 2008 年出版了中英對照本，書名“聊齋故事選”。後來中國與波蘭國進行文化交流，安徽人民出版社把我的這本漢英對照“聊齋故事集”送給了波蘭的文化界，結果在波蘭出版了一本波漢對照版“聊齋故事集”。中國政府有關當局還爲此事發給安徽人民出版社一張嘉獎狀。

因爲我有改寫四十四個聊齋故事爲英文的經驗，所以我能夠“駕輕就熟”地創造了這個怪異奇情故事“天堂遊（A Visit to Heaven）”。所不同的是“聊齋誌異”所寫的都發生於數百年前的古老中國，而我的這篇小說裡所談的則是發生在現代的中國和美國。

事實上，故事就是故事，如果所有的故事都是真實的事情，那就叫做歷史了。而且，事實證明也並不見得所有的歷史書上所說的都是真實的故事。“紅樓夢”的作者曹雪芹說得好，“滿紙荒唐言，一把辛酸淚；都云作者癡，誰解其中味？”因此，也許真正瞭解我這篇小說的“其中味”的人，可能只有“聊齋誌異”的原作者蒲松齡先生了。

還有一件與這篇小說有關係而又非常有趣的事情，我想在此也一併提出。當我在撰寫這篇英文小說時，我參加了休士頓兩個英文寫作批評小組會爲會員。一個是每週四晚間七時至九時開會，開會時每人要帶來不超過五頁的作品，讓大家批判。另一個是每個月的第一及第三個星期三也是晚間七時至九時開會，不過開會時每人可以帶來不超過十頁的作品，讓大家批判。會員有白人也有黑人，除了我以外都是清一色的土生土長美國人。

我記得很清楚當我讀完了我這篇小說的最後一章“作者的筆記”（Author's Notes）時，在每週四的集會中，一個名叫 Helen 的年輕白人女作家（參加會議的人都自認為作家，雖然有些人像我已經有書出版了，可大多數的人還在努力中。）幾乎是拍案而起，她尖銳地叫道，"Tom，我不相信你真的遇到過 James W.Cubin 而且他還到 Houston 來過。你在欺騙你的讀者，將來出版後我是絕對不會買你這本書的。"主持會議的是位年齡比較長也是位白人女作家 Laura，她曾經是美國神秘小說作家協會西南分會的會長，而我也曾經是該分會的正級會員（有神秘小說書出版者），我們感情很好。Laura 微笑著要 Helen 坐下，她說 "這只是 Tom 寫的小說，不是什麼歷史書。"

當我在另一個英文寫作批評小組會上讀完了我這篇小說的最後一章 "作者的筆記"（Author's Notes）時，一個名叫 Steve 的黑人作家緩緩站了起來高聲讚揚這最後一章 "簡直是妙不可言！"

究竟誰是誰非？是 Helen 還是 Steve？親愛的中國讀者朋友們，那就要全評你們的判斷了。

杜　老　伯

（Uncle Du）

前言　Introduction

　　杜老伯於今年年初無疾而終過世了，享壽九十三歲。差不多有一百個人參加了他的追思儀式。可是，可能沒有許多人會知道他的過去如我瞭解他之深。

　　Uncle Du died a natural death at the age of 93 early this year. Nearly one hundred people attended his memorial service, but probably not many of them were as familiar with his past as I was.

　　我認識杜老伯已經有十三、四年了，自 1996 年底我從懷俄明州搬來休士頓後不多久就結識了他。因為我參加了一個本地的佛教團體，這個團體每月固定去訪問幾家多是中國老人居住的公寓。一天，我們去訪問休士頓中國街內的長青公寓，因而認識了杜老伯。他一個人單獨居住在公寓裡，他的妻子已經過世好幾年了。

　　I had known Uncle Du for thirteen or fourteen years since I moved to Houston from Wyoming in the latter part of 1996. I joined a local Chinese Buddhist organization that regularly visited several local apartments where many senior Chinese lived. One day, while visiting Evergreen Apartments in the Chinatown area of Houston, I made the acquaintance of Uncle Du. His wife had died several years earlier and now he lived by himself.

杜老伯不是我的真正伯父，也不是我的任何一個朋友的伯父。因為他是從中國來的長者，依照中國的習慣為表示尊敬，我們都叫他杜老伯，杜是他的姓。

Uncle Du was not my uncle, nor was he related to any one of my friends. Because he was a senior from China, according to the Chinese tradition, we called him Uncle Du as a sign of respect. Du was his family name.

一天下午，在我開車回家的途中，我注意到一位東方老人一手提著一大袋子的食品雜貨緩慢地走在 Corporate Street 馬路邊的人行道上，似乎是由皇朝購貨中心準備去到長青公寓的，而從那裡到公寓還要穿過兩條街。我立刻認出了那個人是杜老伯，乃放慢車速把汽車停靠在他旁邊的馬路上，因為這時附近看不到有其他的車輛往來。我迅速走出汽車叫了聲"杜老伯"，溫和地問他可否讓我帶他回家。他在八十六歲時因為出了兩次大車禍後就不再開車了。當他發現是我時，他笑著說"好的"，便上了我的汽車。

When I was driving home one early afternoon, I noticed an

elderly Oriental man carrying a large bag of groceries in one hand and walking slowly on the sidewalk along Corporate Street. He seemingly was coming from Dynasty Shopping Center and heading toward the Evergreen Apartment that still was a couple of blocks away. I immediately recognized the man as Uncle Du. I slowed down my driving and stopped by his side as the traffic was light without seeing any other vehicles coming or going on that street. Quickly getting out of my car, I addressed him, "Uncle Du," and asked if I could give him a ride home. He quit driving at 86 after having had two major accidents. When he found it was me, he replied, "Okay," with a smile on his face, and he got into my car.

　　到了他的公寓後，他邀請我到他的家中喝杯茶。因爲那天下午沒有什麼事情要做，我高興地接受了他的邀請。我們愉快地談了整整三個鐘頭。從此後，他就時常邀請我到他家喝茶聊天，每次我們都會有個愉快的交談。對我來說，他的過去就好像是一部中國近代史，有的時候也像世界近代史。

After arriving at his apartment, he invited me to have tea at his home. As I had nothing scheduled for that afternoon, I happily accepted his invitation. We shared three hours of pleasant conversation. Since then, he often invited me to have tea at his home and we would have a pleasant chat each time. For me, Uncle Du's past seemed like a study in modern Chinese history, and sometimes a modern world history, too.

他告訴我他明瞭可能不會活得太久了，因爲他已經感覺到身體是一個月比一個月衰弱。他有糖尿病，心臟也有毛病，血壓也很高。當他知道我是個作家，特別喜歡寫近代中國歷史上發生的事跡時，他把他的一生儘可能地詳細告訴了我。他希望在他死後我能將他的一生記錄下來，作爲一個歷史的見證。

He told me that he would probably not be able to live much longer because he was becoming weaker month after month. He suffered from diabetes, heart problem and high blood pressure. When he learned .that I was a writer, especially interested in writing about the events in the modern Chinese history, he told me his life in as much details as he could. He wished I could write his story after his death as a kind of history record in one way or the other.

能夠將杜老伯的一生故事呈現出來實在說是我的光榮。

It is my honor to present Uncle Du, his story and his life.

第一章　Chapter One

杜老伯於九十三年前出生在江蘇省北部灌雲縣內一個名叫前河莊的貧農家中，他的父親姓杜。

Uncle Du was born at a poor farmer's home 93 years ago in China on a farm called Cuan Huo Village, in the County of Guan Yun, the northern part of Jiangsu Province. His father's last name was Du.

　　在那個日子裡，中國的貧農自己沒有土地，向地主租土地來耕種，一半的收成屬於地主，另一半的收成就是這個貧農的全年收入。如果那年收成很好，他和他的家人在那年裡就可以有個簡單日子好過。如果收成不好，那個貧農的全家在那年便會生活得很淒涼了。然而，一個地主往往擁有祖宗傳流下來的好多千畝土地，他不需要親自去田裡工作，不過把他的土地租給上百個佃戶去耕種，去坐收那一半的收成。因此，一個富裕的地主永遠是富裕的，而一個貧農永遠是貧窮。數千年來的中國一直是如此的一直到 1949 年，中國共產黨佔領了整個的中國，將所有地主的土地沒收為國有。

　　In those days in China, a poor farmer owned no land, but rented land from a landlord to farm, sharing half of the harvest with his landlord. As the other half of harvest was the farmer's only income for the whole year, if he had a good harvest, he and his family would make a simple living that year. If not, the poor farmer and his family would live a miserable and hungry life in the whole year. But a landlord often owned many thousand acres of land, inherited from his ancestors. He did not have to work in the field, but lent his land to hundreds of farmers and collected half of each tenant's harvest. Therefore, a rich landlord was always rich while a poor farmer was always poor. That had been the situation for thousands of years in China until 1949, when the Chinese Communists occupied the whole China mainland and confiscated all of the land from the landlords.

　　杜老伯的父母親便是這麼樣的兩個貧窮農夫。他是他父母的唯一小孩。長大後，他成為一個聰明英俊的少年。他的父親明瞭如果不讓他接受好的教育，他的兒子長大後便只能會和他及他的祖宗們一樣地在田地裡耕種一輩子，永遠貧窮而沒有機會改善生活水準。在那個時代的中國農村裡還沒有公共學堂的設立。杜老伯的父親懇求他的地主周先生，能否讓他的兒子有個機會在地主家僱請的家庭教師教導他的孩子們的班上跟著附讀，他的兒子可以擔任教室裡的書童，不要工錢，可也不必付學費。

Uncle Du's parents were two of those poor farmers. He was his parents' only child. When he grew older, he turned out to be a smart and handsome young man. His father realized that without a good education, his son would have to work in the field all of his life like what he and his ancestors had done and remain poor without a chance to raise his living conditions. There were no public schools those days in the remote country areas in China, so Uncle Du's father begged his landlord, Mr. Chou, if he could let his son also have a chance to study from the tutor whom the landlord hired to teach his children at his home. His son could work as a classroom servitor without salary in trade for not paying the tuition.

　　開始時，周先生並不想接受他的佃戶的請求；但當他發現這個年輕人的聰明英俊像貌時，認爲與其他佃戶們的孩子們是完全不同，而他也的確需要一個書童，於是他改變主意，接受了這個貧農的請求。

In the beginning, Mr. Chou did not want to accept his tenant's request. But after viewing how smart and handsome the young man looked, totally different from his other tenants' children, and because he did need a classroom servitor, he changed his mind and gave his okay to the poor farmer.

家庭教師姓鄭，是省裡唯一一所專科學校的畢業生。鄭先生教導地主的三個孩子，兩個男孩，復漢和復剛，一個女孩，復琳。

The tutor's last name was Zen, a graduate of the only junior college in the province. Mr. Zen tutored the landlord's three children, two boys, Fu-han and Fu-gang, and one girl, Fu-lin.

在那個年代裡，沒有受過教育的貧窮人家孩子們是沒有名字的，不過叫做小毛頭或小丫頭（意思就是 "低賤的小男孩" 或 "低賤的小女孩"）。現在，這個杜家的小毛頭也要接受正規教育了，鄭先生乃給這個小男孩起了一個名字，"大業"。"大" 就是光大，"業" 就是行業，希望這個男孩長大後，也能光大他的行業。

In those days, the poor people's uneducated children usually had no first names but was called Xou Mao Tou or Xou

Ya Tou, literally "humble little boy" or "humble little girl"..
Now that the Xou Mao Tou of Du's family was going to receive
a formal education, Mr. Zen gave the little boy a first name,
Da-ye. Da means "glorify" and Ye means "career", hoping that
the boy would glorify his career when he grew up.

第二章　Chapter Two

　　地主的兩個男孩復漢和復剛很不喜歡讀書。大業深深知
道他能接受這個教育的機會來得很不容易，所以他拼命地努
力讀書。復琳是個美麗聰明的女孩，她和大業一樣地喜歡讀
書。漸漸地，大業和復琳的學業進步得很快，而復漢和復剛
兩人則沒有什麼進步。這兩個貴公子嫉妒大業的進步，時常
故意找大業的麻煩，不是說他的服務不好，就是說沒有把教
室打掃乾淨。每當這種情況發生時，復琳就挺身而出為大業
辯護說她的兩位哥哥說的話不實在。

　　The landlord's two boys, Fu-han and Fu-gang, did not like
to study. Because Da-ye deeply realized that it was not easy for
him to have a chance to receive an education, he studied as hard
as he could. Fu-lin was a pretty and smart girl. She enjoyed
studying as much as Da-ye. Gradually, Da-ye and Fu-lin made
extraordinary progress while Fu-han and Fu-gang languished in
their studies. Being jealous of Da-ye's progress, the two rich
boys often found some excuses to blame Da-ye either for his
not doing a good service to them or not cleaning the classroom

well enough. Every time this happened, Fu-lin would speak up for Da-ye, defending him against her brothers' false accusations.

數年後，大業和復琳墜入了愛河。他出身於貧窮人家，而她則是家庭富裕，是不可能獲得雙方父母的同意去結秦晉之好的，他們對此非常明瞭，所以他們只能在暗中相互關懷。他們的親密友誼與日俱增。終於，復漢和復剛將大業和復琳的相愛報告了他們的父母。這個富裕的地主大為震怒，他把大業趕出教室，命令他回去和他的父母一起種田。

Several years later, Da-ye and Fu-lin fell in love. Because he was from a poor family while her family was wealthy, it was impossible for them to get their parents' approval of marriage. They both realized it. So all they did was secretly caring for each other as much as they could. Their intimate friendship became stronger as time passed. Finally, Fu-han and Fu-gang reported to their parents about Fu-lin and Da-ye's love. The rich landlord was furious. He demanded that Da-ye get out of the classroom and ordered him to go back to work with his parents in the field.

大業被趕出教室後，復琳絕食抗議。她勇敢地公開告訴父母她愛大業，而他也愛她，她要和他結婚。假如她的父母不批准她們的婚姻，她說她要去自殺。她的反抗使得周先生大怒，他不理會女兒的恐嚇。

After Da-ye was ordered out of school, Fu-lin refused to eat in protest. She openly and bravely told her parents that she loved Da-ye and he loved her, too. She wanted to marry him. If her parents did not approve the marriage, she said she would commit suicide. Her rebellion made Mr. Chou very angry. He dismissed his daughter's threat as not serious.

數天後，復琳的母親發現女兒因為絕食的原因健康情況一天比一天惡劣。做母親的乃暗裡將女兒的情況與她的丈夫研究並提醒他，如果撇開他的貧窮家庭背景不談，大業實在是個良好的青年。終於，這位固執的父親假裝屈服了。他讓大業回到教室，並同意女兒和大業訂婚，不過他告訴他的女兒，她和大業要結婚實在太年輕了。那年，大業十六歲，復琳十五歲。

A few days later, Fu-lin's mother discovered that her daughter's physical condition was becoming worse daily due to starvation. The mother secretly discussed her daughter's condition with her husband. She strongly reminded him that Da-ye was truly a very nice young man if they could ignore his poor family's background. Finally, the stubborn father pretended to give in. He let Da-ye return to the classroom and also approved his daughter's engagement with Da-ye. But he told his daughter that she and Da-ye were too young to get married. Da-ye was 16 and Fu-lin was 15 that year.

　　與復琳訂婚數個月後，大業被一個當地的軍閥抽去當兵，送到前線去和另一個軍閥打仗。在那個時代裡，中國有很多的軍閥。因爲中央政府太軟弱無法控制這個龐大的國家，軍閥們相互爭打不休。富裕的人家賄賂軍閥使他們的兒子們不被抽去當兵。也許是復琳的父親故意玩弄的手法，讓軍閥把大業抽去當兵的；至少他沒有爲大業去賄賂軍閥。大業離開家鄉去到戰場，復琳傷心欲絕，她痛哭了好幾天。她的父親向她解釋他實在是沒有能力去防止這種事情發生。

　　Several months after his engagement to Fu-lin, Da-ye was drafted by a local warlord and sent to the battlefield in a war against another warlord. In those years, there were many warlords in China. They fought against each other constantly while the central government was too weak to control the huge nation. Wealthy people bribed the warlords so their sons would not be drafted. Maybe it was Fu-lin's father's trick that he purposely let the warlord draft Da-ye, or at least he did not bribe the warlord for Da-ye. Either way Da-ye left home for the battlefield. Fu-lin was heartbroken. She cried for several days. Her father explained to her that he could do nothing to prevent it from happening.

　　戰爭於兩年後結束時，大業跑回家去，驚訝地發現他的未婚妻復琳早已被她的父親強迫嫁給一個富裕的青年了，她的父親告訴她大業已經在戰場上犧牲了。這件事情發生在一九三零年代的後期。

When the war ended two years later, Da-ye rushed home and surprisingly found that his fiancee, Fu-lin, had already been forced by her father to marry a wealthy young man, after telling her that Da-ye had been killed in the battlefield. This happened in the late 1930s.

第三章 Chapter Three

大業非常懊惱，可是他沒有能力把事實反轉過來。他不想再在家中停留了，乃到中國的南方參加蔣介石領導下的國民黨軍隊，進入了黃埔軍官學校做個學生。一年畢業後，他被派去前線作戰希望能消滅軍閥使中國再度有一個強有力的中央政府。

Da-ye was upset. But he could do nothing to reverse the situation. He did not want to stay at home anymore and went to the southern part of China to join the Nationalist army under the leadership of Chiang Kai-shek and enrolled with the Nationalist's Huang Pu Military Academy as a student. After graduation a year later, he was sent to the battlefields in a war to destroy all of the warlords in order to bring China under one powerful central government again.

半年後，他負傷被送去一家軍醫院治療。在醫院裡，他與一位名叫王玉梅的軍中女護士相愛。在那個情況下他們是不可能結婚的，大業與玉梅私訂終身，發誓戰爭結束後就立刻結婚。身體復原後，大業又回到了戰場。

Half a year later he was injured and transferred to a military hospital for treatment. While in the hospital, he and a female military medical nurse named Yu-mei Wang fell in love. But the circumstance could not allow them to get married. Da-ye and Yu-mei were engaged privately, vowing that they would get married whenever the war was over. After he recovered, Da-ye was sent back to the battlefield.

當蔣介石的國民黨軍隊統一了全國後，日本的軍隊無情地侵略中國。大業又被派去從一個戰場到另一個戰場抵抗日本的侵略。

When Chiang Kai-shek's Nationalist army finally united the whole nation, the Japanese military troops mercilessly invaded China. Da-ye had to follow his troops fighting against the Japanese invasion from one battlefield to the other.

1941 年 12 月 7 日，日本戰機特襲美國在太平洋最大的海軍基地珍珠港，使美國的海軍遭受了巨大的損失。第二天，美國宣佈對日戰爭，中日之戰終於發展爲二次世界大戰。

December 7, 1941, the Japanese warplanes carried out a surprised air raid on Pearl Harbor, the largest US naval base in the Pacific, causing a tremendous loss on the American navy. The following day, the United States declared war on Japan. The Sino-Japanese War finally evolved into Second World War.

　　當戰爭於 1945 年結束時，大業是時官階陸軍少校，申請提早自軍中退休，他計劃與玉梅結婚後帶著她回到他的老家去務農一生。殊不知此時的中國共產黨軍隊已經日益強壯，企圖從蔣介石的手中佔領整個的中國大陸，於是，一場巨大的內戰開始了。大業的家鄉江蘇省很快地落入共產黨之手，所以他變得無家可歸。同時，他又實在找不到一個滿意的養家活口工作。在這種情況下，他乃延緩與玉梅結婚的計劃，重新投入國民黨軍隊與共產黨軍作戰。

　　When the War at last ended in 1945, Da-ye, by now holding the rank of major, took an early retirement from the army. He planned to marry Yu-mei and take her to his native province to start over as a farmer for the rest of his life. But unexpectedly by this time, the Chinese Communist troops had already strengthened and attempted to wrestle control of the whole China mainland from Chiang Kai-shek's Nationalists leading to the nation's big civil war. Da-ye's native province, Jiangsu, was soon lost to the hands of Communists so he had no home to return to. And he could not find a satisfactory job to support a family. Under these circumstances, he postponed his marriage to Yu-mei and rejoined the Nationalist's army fighting against the Communists.

　　僅僅數年間，共產黨軍打敗了國民黨軍隊佔領了差不多整個的中國大陸。一時很多的中國人民都想離開大陸去到一個安全的地方。大業的未婚妻玉梅計劃跟隨她的父母與蔣介石的國民黨政府一同撤退去臺灣，這時大業和他的軍隊還在大陸與共產黨軍進行一場最後的戰爭。兩個情人見面商討他們的未來，談了一整天也沒有獲得一個較好的結論。玉梅眼淚汪汪地告訴大業她會在臺灣等他，大業答允玉梅他一定會儘快去那裡和她團聚，然後他們就在島上結婚建立他們甜蜜的家園。

In only a few years, the Communists defeated the Nationalist troops taking over just about the whole China mainland. Many Chinese tried to leave the mainland for a safer place. Da-ye's fiancee, Yu-mei, planned to follow her parents to flee to Taiwan along with the retreat of Chiang Kai-shek's Nationalist government while Da-ye and his troops were still fighting in the last battlefield against the Communists. The two lovers met and discussed about their future all day long but could not think of any concrete options. Yu-mei tearfully told Da-ye that she would wait for him in Taiwan. Da-ye promised her that he would join her there as soon as he could. Then they would marry and build a sweet home on the island.

兩個月後，國民黨軍隊與共產黨軍的最後一戰結束了，國民黨在大陸上的軍隊完全被消滅，大業和很多其他的國民黨軍官都變成了戰俘。雖然他們很快被釋放了，可是大業沒有任何辦法溜出大陸到臺灣去，而只好停留在那裡和其他的人們一樣找個工作生活下去。從此，大業和玉梅就完全失掉了聯繫。無情的戰爭把成千上萬的中國家庭分散在中國大陸及臺灣島兩處，數十年來都不知道對方是死還是活著。

Two months later, the last battle between the Nationalists and the Communists ended and the Nationalist's army on the China mainland was totally destroyed. Da-ye and many other Nationalist military officers became prisoners of war. Although they were soon released, Da-ye had no way to sneak out of the mainland for Taiwan but stayed to find a job making a living like everybody else. Since then, Da-ye and Yu-mei had lost contact completely. The merciless war divided hundred of thousands of Chinese families in two places, the China mainland and the island of Taiwan, without knowing the other families alive or dead for many decades.

第四章　Chapter Four

　　1950 年 6 月 25 日，北韓陸軍突然向南韓發動攻擊。不久，美國五星上將道格那斯、麥克亞瑟被美國總統杜魯門派爲聯合國軍總司令，幫助南韓反擊北韓，於是韓戰開始。當北韓軍隊被擊得節節敗退時，中國共產黨主席毛澤東迅速組織了個百萬人的所謂中國人民志願軍，開赴韓國戰場幫助北韓攻打聯合國軍。

On June 25, 1950, the North Korean army launched a surprised attack on South Korea. Soon American 5-Star General Douglas MacArthur was appointed by American President Truman to be the commander-in-chief of the United Nations' allied troops to help the South Korea fight against the North Korea, and the Korean War started. When North Korea was being defeated, Mao Ze-Dong of the Chinese Communist chairman hurriedly organized a so-called Chinese Voluntary Army of one million soldiers and sent them to the Korean battlefield helping the North Korea fight against the U.N. allied troops.

為了表達對新中國的忠貞，大業參加了中國人民志願軍去到韓國戰場，為中國共產黨打擊美國領導的聯合國軍隊。

To show his loyalty to the new China, Da-ye joined the Chinese Voluntary Army. He was sent to the Korean battlefield for the Chinese Communists to fight against the US led allied troops.

一年後，大業和很多其他的中國士兵被聯合國軍隊俘虜。當雙方研究交換軍俘時，一些中國俘虜表明意願去臺灣而不願意回去中國。大業就是其中之一個。這是一九五四年一月間的事情。

A year later, Da-ye and many other Chinese soldiers were captured by the U.N. allied troops. When the two sides negotiated to exchange the prisoners of war, some Chinese prisoners expressed their willingness to go to Taiwan instead of China. Da-ye was one of them. It happened in January 1954.

　　到了臺灣後，大業發現他的未婚妻那個護士王玉梅早已
經和一個醫生結了婚，而且有了一男一女兩個小孩。因爲這
麼多年沒有任何關於他的生死存亡消息，她推測他可能早已
在戰場上陣亡了。在這場多年的巨大政治混亂中，這種事情
經常發生，大業不去責怪玉梅。

After reaching Taiwan, Da-ye found that his fiancee,
Yu-mei Wang, the medical nurse, had married a medical doctor
and already had two children, one boy and one girl. With no
information about his life or death for so many years, she
presumed that he must have been killed in battle. It was very
common during those years of political chaos. Da-ye did not
blame Yu-mei.

第五章　Chapter Five

　　由於大業此時仍很年輕不過三十出頭四十還不到，當他
在臺灣一切安頓下來後，他仍去一個私立學院讀書。畢業後，
很幸運地獲得一個基督教團體的幫助，他來到美國留學，註
冊於密歇根州安阿博市的密歇根大學，主修會計副修經濟。

As Da-ye was still young in his late 30s, after settling
down in Taiwan, he went back to school registering with a
private college. After graduation, with the help of a Christian
organization, he luckily came to the United States for advanced
studies.　He registered himself with the University of
Michigan in Ann Arbor, Michigan, majoring in accounting with

a minor in economics.

　　一年後，他與同班的美國同學 Mary Jones 戀愛。Mary
的父親 John Jones 曾經參加二次世界大戰，在中國成都美國
將軍陳納德的飛虎隊中擔任戰機駕駛員，幫助中國政府抵抗
日軍。這位美國退伍軍人要他的女兒邀請大業來家晚飯，兩
個男子談到戰爭的往事很快變成了朋友。John 鼓勵他的女兒
接受大業爲她的男朋友。當大業獲得碩士學位在 Ann Arbor
一家很大的建築公司 Style Home Builder 裡得到一個會計職
位後，他便與 Mary 結婚，計劃在美國長期居留。三年後，
他歸化爲美國公民。

　　A year later, he fell in love with his American classmate,
Mary Jones. Mary's father, John Jones, had joined the Second
World War helping the Chinese government fight against the
Japanese in Cen-Du, China, under American General
Chennault's Flying Tigers as a warplane pilot. The ex-American
service man asked his daughter to invite Da-ye home for dinner.
The two men explored their war involvement and soon became
friends. John encouraged his daughter to accept Da-ye as her
boyfriend. When Da-ye earned his master's degree and found a
job with a large construction company, Style Home Builders, in
Ann Arbor as an accountant, he married Mary and decided to
stay in the United States. Three years later, he became
naturalized as a US citizen.

　　數年後，大業服務的 Style Home Builder 因爲經營不善，終於關門了。雖然多方努力，可大業就是找不到另一個滿意的工作。這個時候，美國已經捲入越戰好幾年了。大業的一個密歇根大學要好的同班同學 Jack Clark 已被任命爲西貢美國大使館裡的經濟參事。Jack 邀請大業去做他的助手。因爲大業的背景，Jack 肯定大業一定會被大使重用的，大業非常興奮。

　　A few years later, because of bad management, Style Home Builders, the company Da-ye worked with, went out of business. As hard as he tried, Da-ye could not find another satisfactory job. By this time, the United States had been involved with the Vietnam War for several years. One of Da-ye's close classmates at the University of Michigan, Jack Clark, was appointed as the economic counselor in the American embassy in Saigon. Jack invited Da-ye to work with him as his assistant. Because of Da-ye's background, Jack was sure Da-ye would be highly welcome by the ambassador. Da-ye was excited.

　　他與 Mary 商討，她強烈反對這個主意，她說她寧願和他離婚也不願去西貢。事實上，Mary 和大業早已經發現了他們生活上的矛盾，很少親戚朋友們會相信他們能夠愉快地白首到老的。於是，他們沒有什麼爭論便辦妥了離婚手續，離婚後大業就去西貢就任他的新職了。

　　He consulted with Mary. She was strongly against this idea,

declaring that she would rather divorce him instead of going to Saigon. The fact was that Mary and De-ye had already found their differences in their ways of living. Few of their relatives and friends believed that the couple would live happily together for the rest of their lives. So they divorced without much argument or unhappiness. After that, Da-ye went to Saigon to take his new job.

第六章　Chapter Six

Jack 的話一點兒不錯，因為大業的身世和他現在已經是個美國公民，美國大使在大業到達西貢的當天就邀請 Jack 和大業到他的官邸晚餐。從此，大使就時常和大業商談如何應付當地的越南與中國權貴們。在那個時代的越南，主要的軍政職位都是由越南人士擔任，而富裕的中國移民就控制了所有經濟方面的命脈。在西貢的高級社交圈子裡，大業經常被越南和中國權貴們邀請去參加他們的聚會，而被待若上賓。

Jack was right. Because of Da-ye's background and experiences and now he was a US citizen, the American ambassador invited Jack and Da-ye to have dinner at his official residence on the day Da-ye arrived in Saigon. Since then, the ambassador had often discussed with Da-ye on the issues of how to deal with the dignities of local Vietnamese and Chinese. In those years in South Vietnam, the native Vietnamese held all the major political and military positions while the wealthy

Chinese immigrants were in control of all the key businesses. Da-ye was often invited by the Vietnamese and the Chinese dignitaries to attend their parties and he was always treated as a VIP in the Saigon's high social circles.

　　不久，他結識了一位富裕的女商人，李麗麗。麗麗是第三代移民越南的華裔。她美麗、能幹，三十出頭，能操流利的越南話、中國話及英語。她的丈夫是個聞名的華裔越南銀行家，他在越南擁有好幾家銀行。在一場與北越的戰鬥中，這位銀行家不幸意外中彈，當被送去醫院急診室後，不久就過世了。

Soon he made the acquaintance of a wealthy businesswoman, Lily Lee. Lily was the third generation of Chinese immigrant in Vietnam. She was a pretty and capable woman in her early 30s, speaking fluent Vietnamese, Chinese and English. Her husband was a well-known Chinese-Vietnamese banker who owned many banks in South Vietnam. During a battle with the North, the banker was accidentally shot and died soon after being sent to an emergency room.

　　由於麗麗在西貢的高級社交圈子裡非常活躍，她與大業經常在很多場合中碰頭。當她發現大業與美國大使的親密關係後，她故意不時地邀請大業去她那豪華的住宅晚餐。日子久了，他們墜入了愛河。一年後他們結婚了，包括美國大使在內有數百位越南、中國及美國權貴們參加了他們的婚禮，這在當年的西貢高級社交圈子中算是一件大事。

As Lily was very active in the high society in Saigon, she and Da-ye often met on many occasions. When she discovered Da-ye's close relationship with the American ambassador, she purposely invited Da-ye to have dinner at her luxurious home as often as could. Gradually, they fell in love. When they were married a year later, hundreds of Vietnamese, Chinese and American dignitaries, including the American ambassador, attended their wedding ceremony. It was a big event in Saigon's high social activities.

由於越戰拖延已經有數年之久，在國內的巨大壓力下，尼克森總統於 1972 年 12 月中旬開始將美國軍隊從越南戰場上撤回國內。大業與麗麗預測這場戰爭將不會有個好的收場。夫妻兩人商討結果，她將她的銀行全部售出，他將他大使館中的職位辭去，大業把他的妻子帶回了美國。

By this time the Vietnam War had dragged on for several years. Under heavy domestic pressure in the mainland, in the middle of December 1972, President Nixon started to withdraw US ground troops from the Vietnamese battlefields. Da-ye and Lily predicted that the war was going to produce no favorable end. After discussion, she sold all of her banks and he resigned his job with the American embassy. Da-ye brought his wife back to the States.

第七章　Chapter Seven

有了三百萬元現金在手中，他們在科羅拉多州丹佛市先行定居。經過了數個月的觀察，他們買下了丹佛市中心的一家五星級 275 個房間的連鎖旅館假日旅舍，百分之十頭款兩百五十萬元是麗麗從越南帶回來的。

With three million dollars cash on hand, they settled in Denver, Colorado. After a few months of studies, they bought a franchised 5-star 275-room full service Holiday Inn Hotel in downtown Denver with ten percent down of payment, two and half million dollars, which Lily brought from Vietnam.

接收手續完畢後，大業與麗麗挽留所有的員工，召開多次會議宣達他們新的經營方針。

After becoming the owners, Da-ye and Lily held a series of meetings with their employees, whom they kept from the previous owners, to publicize their new management policies.

第一個規定：發動“微笑”運動。員工們與顧客接觸時，不管這個顧客是如何地不講情理，臉上必須永遠掛著微笑。

Rule Number One: They launched a "smile" policy. Employees were to keep a smile on their faces when dealing with guests, no matter how unreasonable the guest was.

　　第二個規定：不管在何種情況下，都不要對顧客說
"不"字。如果這個顧客的要求是實在無法接受的話，可以
說，"你是對的，不過……"

Rule Number Two: Employees were to never say "No" to a
guest under any situations but were instructed to say "You are
right, but......" if the guest's request was unacceptable.

　　第三個規定：當一個顧客要求退回訂金時，即使會使旅
館造成損失，也不可以問原因而必須立刻退費。大業和麗麗
解釋道從長遠的角度來看，這個顧客一定會毫不猶豫地再定
房間的。

Rule Number Three: Employees were to refund a guest's
deposit without asking reason even if doing so would result in a
financial loss. Da-Ye and Lily explained that, over time, the
guest was likely not to hesitate to book a room again.

　　為了執行上面的營業方針，夫婦兩人給予他們的員工很
多獎賞項目。

In order to carry out the above policies, the couple created
many programs to recognize their employees with rewards or
promotions.

　　一年後，大業和麗麗的旅館生意蒸蒸日上，利潤也跟著
大為增加。當他們聽到在鄰近不遠處鹽湖城有一家連鎖旅館
假日旅舍出售時，他們向他們的銀行貸款把它買了下來。在

這以後的四年內，他們又購買了位於中西部的另外三家連鎖
旅館假日旅舍。

A year later Da-ye and Lily's hotel business flourished and
their profit increased sharply. When they heard of another
franchised Holiday Inn hotel for sale in nearby Salt Lake City,
they took out a loan with their bank and purchased it. In the
following four years, they purchased three more Holiday Inn
hotels, all in the Midwest states.

*"假如我們的旅館生意能夠一直這樣順利發展下去的
話，十到十五年間，我們就可以成為千萬富豪了，"* 大業與
麗麗愉快地相互慶賀道。然而，事情之發展並不如他們所預
期的順利。

*If our hotel business continues to be profitable like this,
we'll become billionaires in ten* to *fifteen years,* Da-ye and Lily
happily told each other. But things did not work as well as they
predicted.

首先，一個有名望的女性客人在他們的鹽湖城旅館房間
裡被強姦了。這個女人控告旅館主人疏忽罪，官司打了兩年，
結果法官判決大業和麗麗輸了，他們必須賠償這個女人三百
五十萬元。

First, a well-known female customer was raped at their
Salt Lake City hotel room. The woman sued the owners of hotel
for neglect. The law battle lasted for two years. A judge finally

ruled against Da-ye and Lily and ordered that they pay the woman three and half million dollars.

第二，由於在以往數年中中西部蓋了很多的新旅館，激烈的競爭結果，使得他們的營業額逐年減少差不多百分之十。

Second, because of large numbers of new hotels opening in the Midwest states over the next few years, the keen competition caused their room bookings to decrease about ten percent each year.

最後，大業和麗麗對於按月如期繳付巨額貸款感到緊張，而日子一久事情也就愈來愈糟糕。在這種強大的經濟壓力情況下，他們與他們的律師們研究結果，發現委實無路可走，只有依據破產法第七章規定申請破產，這就是說他們不必再去擔心他們的債務了，可是，他們喪失了他們的全部旅館了。因爲她的所有財富都沒有了，麗麗痛哭了整整一個禮拜。惡運不僅粉碎了他們的千萬富豪美夢，那更煩惱的是大業必須再去法庭，因爲麗麗又在這個時候要求和他離婚。

Finally, Da-ye and Lily found they were unable to pay their heavy monthly mortgage payments on time, and things grew worse for them as time went on. Under such a strong financial pressure, they consulted with their lawyers and had no option but to file for bankruptcy under Chapter Seven. It meant that they would not have to pay their debtors anymore, but they lost all of their hotels. Lily cried for an entire week because all of her fortune was gone. The bad fortune not only crushed their billionaire dream but also made Da-ye go to the court again as Lily filed for divorce.

第八章　Chapter Eight

　　離婚後，大業又變成單身了。他搬到了德州休士頓，在一家建築公司裡擔任會計，這是他多年前於密西根大學畢業後所獲得的一個同樣職位。

After his divorce, Da-ye became single again. He moved to Houston, Texas and found work with a construction company as an accountant, the same type of job he had taken after he graduated from University of Michigan many years ago.

　　由於休士頓的生活程度比國內其他很多大都市要低得多，不數年間，他積存下了兩萬元。

Because the living standard in Houston was much lower than most of the other metropolises in the country, in a few years, Da-ye saved up twenty thousand dollars.

　　自從尼克森總統於 1972 年訪問中國以後，中國開始將它的閉關自守政策轉變爲對外開放，中美兩國在對方的首都各自設立聯絡辦事處。1976 年毛澤東過世後，副總理鄧小平掌握了實權。鄧讓居住中國境外的華人可以回去探望他們的親人。

After President Nixon's visit to China in 1972, China began to change its policy from one of obscurity to one of openness. China and the U.S. opened liaison offices in each other's capitals. After Mao Ze-dong died in 1976, Vice Premier Deng Xiaoping consolidated his power. Deng let the Chinese people living outside of China return to visit their relatives.

大業離開中國已經有好幾十年了，他立刻從華府的中國聯絡辦事處那裡取得了簽證，回到了他的故鄉江蘇省的北方。他悲痛地發現不僅他的父母親就是那年邁的地主周先生夫婦也都早已過世多年了。甚至於周先生的兩個兒子復漢和復剛也在文化大革命運動中死亡了。唯一他兒時所認識而如今仍尚存活的人就是復琳，那個他在十七歲時曾經和她訂過親的女人。她在大業被抽去當兵打仗的時候，被她的父親欺騙和強迫嫁給了一個有錢的男子。她的丈夫也在文化大革命時間遇害了，他們沒有小孩。當大業在復琳家中和她相見時，她簡直不能相信這是個事實。這是他們十五、六歲時分別後的第一次見面，現在，他是六十歲，她是五十九。

Da-ye had left China for several decades. He immediately applied for a visa from the Chinese Liaison Office in Washington, D.C. and returned to his native place in the northern Jiang-su Province. He was very sad to find that not only his parents but also his aged landlord, Mr. Chow, and his wife had all died years earlier. Even Mr. Chow's two sons, Fu-han and Fu-gang, had both died in the Great Proletarian

Cultural Revolution. The only person whom he had known in his childhood and still survived was Fu-lin, the woman he had once been engaged to when he was 16. She had been cheated and forced to marry a wealthy man by her father while Da-ye was drafted to go to the battlefield. Now her husband had also died in the Revolution, and they had no children. When Da-ye met Fu-lin at her home, she could not believe it was a reality. It was the first time for them to meet each other again since they were middle teenagers. Now he was 60 and she was 59.

"啊，大業，我們是不是在做夢？"她問他，她的喜悅的眼淚順著她的雙頰流個不停。

"Oh, Da-ye, are we in a dream?" she asked him while her joyful tears running down along her cheeks endlessly.

"不是的，復琳，我們不是在夢中。我們都經歷了千辛萬苦，現在自由了，我們在我們出生的地方相遇和談話。"大業向她保證，把她的兩隻手緊緊地握著。

"No, Fu-lin, we are not in a dream. We both have survived many difficult times. Now we are free to meet and talk in the place we were born," Da-ye assured her, holding her both hands tightly.

大業和復琳相聚三日，然後帶著她漫遊北京、南京、西安等很多歷史性的都市。雖然復琳住在中國，可她從來沒有

錢去遊玩這些地方。在首先的兩天夜晚裡，他們仍然在大業
預定的兩個不同的旅館房間裡休息。

Da-ye stayed with Fu-lin for three days, then took her to
visit Beijing, Nanjing, Xian, and many other Chinese historical
cities where Fu-lin had never had money to go even though she
lived in China. In the first two days, when they went to a hotel
to rest in the evening, Da-ye still booked two separate rooms
for them.

在第三天晚間，他們兩人於晚餐時都喝了很多杯的中國
烈酒，大業把復琳留在他的房間裡過夜，他們終於發生了性
行為。

In the third evening, after both of them had consumed
many cups of Chinese whiskey during the dinner, Da-ye kept
Fu-lin in his room, and they finally made love.

第二天早晨，他要求她嫁給他，她突然哭泣了起來，她
告訴他，"我等待這快樂的一刻已經等了很多很多的年了。"

The next morning, when he asked her to marry him, she
suddenly cried. Then she told him, "I have waited for such a
happy moment for many, many years!"

大業與他的兒時情侶復琳結婚了，只有她的少數鄰居們
參加了他們的簡單婚禮。婚後，他把她帶回了美國。雖然大
業已經不是百萬富翁了，可他們仍然生活得非常愉快和平

安。兩個老人終於在這塊新大陸上享受到了美滿的婚姻　。

So, Da-ye married his childhood sweetheart, Fu-lin, with only a handful of her neighbors attending their simple wedding ceremony. After marriage, he brought her back to the United States. Although Da-ye was not a millionaire now, they lived happily and peacefully. The two seniors finally enjoyed their conjugal happiness in the new land.

大業六十五歲時，他辭去了建築公司的工作，申請退休，然後把他們的小房子賣了，搬到中國街附近專門為中國老人建築居住的長青公寓。

When Da-ye was sixty-five years old, he resigned his job with the construction company and applied for retirement. They sold their small house and moved to an apartment, Evergreen Village, a complex especially built for the senior Chinese to live in the Chinatown area.

1995 年，他的妻子死於肝癌。從此，他就一直是一個人居住。現在，大家都知道的杜老伯杜大業也過世了。

In 1995, Fu-lin died of liver cancer. From that on, he lived by himself. Now Da-ye Du, known to everyone as Uncle Du, was gone also.

後記　Author's Notes

在他的 93 年生涯裡，杜老伯曾經參加過很多次戰爭：中國早期的軍閥們內戰，抵抗日本侵略的二次世界大戰，國共兩黨間的內戰，幫助北韓抵抗聯合國軍的韓戰，又目睹了美國幫助南越抵抗中國共產黨支持北越的越戰。

In his 93 years of life, Uncle Du had actually attended many wars - the civil war between warlords in early China, the Second World War of defending China from the Japanese invasion, the civil war between the Nationalist Chinese government and the Chinese Communists, the Korean War helping the North Korea fight against the U.S. led United Nations allied troops, and he eye-witnessed the Vietnam War with the United States helping South Vietnam fight against North Vietnam supported by the Chinese Communists.

杜老伯原來是個連名字也沒有的一個中國貧農的兒子，可是後來，他又幾乎成爲一個美國千萬富翁。

Uncle Du was a poor Chinese farmer's son without even a first name, but years later he almost became an American billionaire.

他一生共有四個女人：他的第一個情侶周復琳是他的地主的女兒。後來他又和一個女護士王玉梅訂了婚。又後來他和一個美國大學畢業生 Mary Jones 結婚了。離婚後，他又和一個華裔越南職業女人李麗麗結婚。而他最後的女人竟又是他的兒時情侶周復琳。可是，當他在家中因為跌倒被送往醫院急診室時，竟然沒有一個人在他的身邊。

He had had four women in his life. His first sweetheart, Fu-lin Chou, was his landlord's daughter. He and a Chinese female medical nurse, Yu-mei Wang, had become engaged. He had married an American college graduate, Mary Jones. After divorce, he married again with a Chinese-Vietnamese businesswoman, Lily Li. And his last woman was also his first childhood sweetheart, Fu-lin Chou. But when he was rushed to an emergency room after a fall at home, he had no one by his side.

我曾經去過杜老伯的醫院探望他好幾次，如果那天他的精神狀況很好時，我們就會有個愉快的交談。他告訴我在他經歷了這麼多的事件後，除了那些酸甜苦辣的回憶外，他現在是一無所有了。

I visited Uncle Du at the hospital several times and every time we had a pleasant conversation when he felt well. He told me that after having experienced so many events, he now owned nothing, but memories, bitter and sweet mixed.

他於我最後一次探望他後的第三天安祥地過世了。

He passed away peacefully two days after my last visit

with him.

　　是不是我們每一個人都實實在在地擁有世界上一些東西？臺灣的佛教慈濟基金功德會創始人證嚴法師說，沒有人可以擁有任何東西，不過是在世時有權使用而已。

Do we all actually own something in the world? The founder of Buddhist Compassion Relief Tzu Chi Foundation in Taiwan, Rev. Cheng Yen, says that no one owns anything, but merely has the right to use it while alive.

　　因為我有權使用我的筆，我把杜老伯的故事先以英文簡單地寫了出來，放在我的懷俄明州英文報紙，*The Riverton Ranger*，每週專欄上發表了，後來，我又將之翻譯為中文，在德州休士頓的中文報紙，*美南新聞*，上刊出了。現在，我又將他的故事再以英文詳細地重新寫過，放在我 2009 年出版的一本中短篇小說集，*A Visit to Heaven* 中，再度告訴世人杜老伯一生的轟轟烈烈事跡。

While I have the right to use my pen, I concisely wrote Uncle Du's story first in English for my weekly column in an English newspaper, *The Riverton Ranger,* in Wyoming, then I translated my English article into Chinese and had it published by a Chinese newspaper, *Mei Nan Daily News*, in Houston, Texas. Now, I have rewritten his story in English in greater detail for my new book, a collection of short stories, *A Visit to Heaven*, which was published in 2009, telling the world of the many glorious events Uncle Du had experienced in his life.

　　現在，我又將這本英文書翻譯爲中文，在臺灣出版漢英對照本。

Now I have translated this English book into Chinese and have it published in Chinese and English in Taiwan.

　　親愛的杜老伯，請在你的現在世界裡好好安息吧，我已經在我的世界裡把你要我做的事情切實地做到了。

Dear Uncle Du, please take ease in the world you are staying. I have done what you asked me to do in my world.

皮　夾

Wallet

　　王老先生告訴他的妻子、兒子、和兒媳婦，在吃了這麼一頓豐盛的午餐後，他想出去走走，到戶外去好好地散一下步。

Senior Mr. Wang told his wife, son, and daughter-in-law that after such a heavy lunch, he would like to take a walk - a long, slow walk outside of the house.

　　他要他的家人放心，雖然他的英文不行，在這個友善的社區內散步，他有信心一定會平平安安沒有任何問題的。

He assured them that although his English was not good, he was sure that he would be all right during the walk in this friendly neighborhood.

　　王老原來是臺灣政府中的公務員。他在服務公職四十年期滿後甫於兩個月前辦完了退休手續。雖然已是六十好幾的人了，可仍非常健壯，沒有一般年老人的任何毛病像高血壓糖尿病高膽固醇等等，甚至於連這些病的跡象也一點兒沒有。在體能上，他看起來依然活像一個中年人。他與他的妻子於數週前到美國來探望他們的第三個孩子，亨利，和亨利的妻子玖蒂。這對年輕人住在南加州聖地亞哥的市郊。

Senior Wang used to be a government official in Taiwan. He had just retired a couple of months ago after serving 40 years of public service. Although in his late 60s, he was quite healthy without any of the seniors' common problems such as high blood pressure, diabetes, or high cholesterol, or even slight symptoms of any of them. Physically, he still looked and acted like a middle-aged man. He and his wife came to the United States to visit their third child, Henry, and his wife, Judy, a few weeks earlier. The young couple lived in the suburbs of San Diego, southern California.

這是一個秋日午後，不冷也不熱，是個最適合戶外散步的氣候了。

It was a beautiful fall afternoon, not too hot, or too cold, a perfect weather for a walk outside.

絨毛般的白雲在晴空緩慢地飄動，輕微的陣陣冷風使得這位年長的散步人益發感到說不出來的舒適。王老以他那最輕鬆的步伐悠閑地在順著他兒子住家的街道人行道上走著。穿過了幾條街道後，他看到了一座小型購貨中心，他的兒子和媳婦曾經帶他和他的妻子來這座購貨中心裡面一家叫Safeway 的超級市場買過菜，所以他對這裡的商業環境還算熟悉。

White fluffy clouds wafted lazily overhead in a brilliant azure sky. A gentle cooling breeze added to the senior walker's comfort. Senior Wang tried to relax as much as he wanted strolling leisurely along the sidewalk of the street on which his son's home was located. After a few blocks, he found a small shopping center where his son and daughter-in-law had taken him and his wife to buy groceries at a supermarket called Safeway in the center. He was familiar with this commercial area.

由於感覺有點兒口渴，他乃走進 Safeway 想買一小瓶果汁來喝。在水果飲料部門，他選了一小瓶蘋果汁。他手拿著果汁便排在等候付錢的一個很長的隊伍中。

As he felt a little thirsty, he entered Safeway thinking of buying a small bottle of juice to drink. In the department of fruits and drinks he picked up a small bottle of apple juice. He held the juice in one hand joining a long line of shoppers in front of casher waiting for making his payment.

終於輪到他付錢了，他用右手伸進他長褲後面的右口袋裡去掏皮夾。突然間他發現皮夾不在那裡，他迅速搜索其他的口袋，可都沒有找到。沒有錢付帳，他放棄了飲料，向著收銀員苦笑了一下，把果汁放回原來的架子上。然後他開始思索著如何丟掉了皮夾，很多年來他一直是把皮夾放在褲子後面的那個右邊口袋裡的。

When it was his turn to pay for the juice, he used his right hand to reach his right rear trouser pocket to get his wallet out. Suddenly, he was surprised to find that his wallet was not there. He quickly searched all of his other pockets, but still did not find it. Without money to pay, he gave up on the drink, but made a bitter smile at the cashier and took the bottle of apple juice back on the shelter where he had found it. Then he began to wonder how he had lost the wallet which for several years had always been kept in his right rear trouser pocket.

他重新檢查褲子後面的右口袋，發現口袋上面的鈕釦不見了，明顯地皮夾是滑出去的，也許是被小偷偷去的。他記得他的兒子告訴過他在聖地亞哥市郊經常發生偷竊和搶劫的故事。所以他的皮夾一定是這麼樣地被偷走了的。皮夾裡面還藏有好幾百美元的現鈔，大都是一百元、五十元、及二十元的票面。此外，他的皮夾裡還放有很多重要的文件如兩張信用卡，一張 Master card、一張 Visa，臺灣的駕照、保險卡及醫療卡，以及洛杉磯飛機場移民官員所發給的簽証文書等。現在皮夾沒有了，他簡直無法承受得了丟掉這個皮夾！

He checked the right rear trouser pocket again and discovered the button over it to be loose. Obviously, the wallet was lost or stolen by a thief as he recalled the many stories told by his son about stealing and robbing in San Diego area. He realized that his wallet must have been stolen! There were several hundred US dollars, mostly in 100, 50 and 20 dollar bills, in the wallet. Moreover, his wallet also contained many important documents including his credit cards, a Master Card and a Visa, his Taiwanese driver license and insurance card as well as medical card and the immigration papers issued by the Los Angeles airport immigration officer when they entered this country. But now the wallet was gone. He just could not afford to lose his wallet!

　　另外，這皮夾本身也是他所最喜愛的物品之一，那是他妻子於他們結婚四十週年時送給他的禮品。數年前他在臺灣還沒有退休時，她第一次來美國探望她們的兒子亨利。兒子帶著母親去墨西哥與美國邊境一個名叫 Tijuana 的墨西哥都市遊玩，欣賞一下美國以外的另一個國家風光。她在那裡買了這個皮夾。這是個黑色皮夾外面有手工精製的墨西哥圖案，皮夾呈正方形與美國一般市面上的長方形皮夾不一樣，而且還要大些。

　　Besides, the wallet itself was also one of his most prized possessions as it was given to him by his wife on their 40th wedding anniversary. She had purchased the wallet several years ago in Tijuana, a U.S. border Mexican city when she first visited their son, Henry, who took his mom to see another foreign country besides the United States while senior Wang had not retired in Taiwan at that time. The wallet was made of black leather with delicate hand-made Mexican designs on the outside. It was square different from the rectangle ones sold in the American markets and its size was larger, too.

他非常喜歡這個皮夾，不管去那裡，每天都帶在身上。現在皮夾被偷了，而他連在什麼時候及什麼地方被偷的都毫無所知。他在思考是否要循著來路再尋找一遍。

He loved the wallet so much that he carried it every day wherever he went. Now the wallet was stolen and he could not even realize when and where it happened. He figured whether he must retrace his walk and see if he could find it along the way.

當王老在準備走出這家商店時，他的腦筋裡還在思索著他那心愛的皮夾，他突然湊巧看到了一個黑色頭髮的青年正在櫃檯前付帳，手裡拿著一個黑色正方形皮夾。王老停頓了一下，後退了幾步，集中注意力在這隻皮夾上。他又看到了這個皮夾外面的圖案和他被偷的那個完全一模一樣。是的，他堅信這正是他的皮夾，不久前才發現遺失了的皮夾。這個年輕人一定是偷他皮夾的小偷。現在，這個人用王老的錢付他購買的東西，王老生氣。他考慮去找電話向警察局報案，立刻他想到了這兒是美國不是臺灣，他不通英文如何報案。同時他又害怕即使他會用英文報案，等到員警來到時，這個年輕人一定早已經逃跑了。於是他立刻去接近這個年輕人。這個人已付完了帳正準備離開商店，不經任何考慮他跟著這個人走了出去。

As senior Wang was trying to make his way out of the

store with his mind still on his favorite wallet, he happened to notice a young man with black hair who was paying at the counter holding a black leather square wallet in his hands. Senior Wang stopped for a moment, retreated a few steps and focused on the wallet. He noticed that the wallet even had the same outside design as that of his own. Yes, he was convinced, it was his wallet, the one he had just discovered missing. The young man must be a thief who stole his wallet. Now, the man paid his purchase with senior Wang's money. Senior Wang was angry. He considered to find a telephone to call the police, but he soon remembered he was now in the United Sates not in Taiwan that he had no way to make the report in English, and he was afraid even if he could speak English and make the report, when the police came the young man might have already gotten away. So he immediately approached the young man who had now paid his bill, leaving the store. Without hesitation, he followed the young fellow out.

王老很快發現這個人可能也沒有開車，因爲他正向著購貨中心後面的一條小路上走去。

Senior Wang soon noticed that the young man probably did not have a car either as he was walking toward a narrow lane behind the shopping center.

王老緊跟在這個人的後面。換言之，他在追逐這個年輕人。這個年輕人很快發現了他被人跟蹤了，他開始放快腳步，可王老的腳步也跟著放快。在這條狹窄的路上，除了這兩個一老一少的人在拼命地快步前進外，沒有看到其他任何行人。奇怪的是這兩個人都不說一句話，王老不通英文，所以他閉口不語。這個年輕人似乎也不通英文。王老猜想這個年輕人可能是墨西哥來的新移民，所以英文和他一樣的爛。不過這些不重要，目前他最放在心上的是如何從這個年輕人的手中奪回他的皮夾。

Senior Wang went after the man closely. In another words, he was chasing after the young man. The young man soon discovered that he was being followed. Then he started to walk faster, and senior Wang did so as well. There were no other people in sight on the lone lane other than the two men, one old and one young, walking forward as quickly as they could. Strangely enough, none of the two men spoke a word. Senior Wang did not know English so he kept his mouth shut. It seemed that the young man did not master English either. From his black hair, it was very possible that he might be a newly arrived Mexican immigrant; therefore, his English might be as poor as his, senior Wang thought. Well, that was not important. All that he was concerned about right now was how to get his wallet back from the young man.

這個人開始快步跑了，王老也跟在後面跑。幸虧這個人因為跑急跌了一覺，這讓王老又跟上了。這個時候，這個人看來很緊張也很懼怕。雖然，王老還是不知道下一步怎麼走，如何從這個人的手裡弄回他丟失的皮夾。

Then the man began to run fast, and so did senior Wang. Luckily, the man stumbled and fell allowing senior Wang easily caught up to him. The man now looked nervous and scared. Still, senior Wang did not know how to do next, to get his lost wallet back from the man.

突然間，王老想起了已故的華裔美國電影明星李小龍及他在功夫電影中用中國武術去打擊罪犯的故事。既然這個年輕人拿著他的皮夾，這個年輕人一定是個罪犯。因為王老在年輕時也曾經學習過一些武術，也許因為他太過高估了他的武術，說時遲那時快，他乃以極其快速的動作衝跳到這個年輕男子的前面使其停步不動，並仿照李小龍電影裡的動作擺出了一個漂亮的功夫架子。隨後他以右手不停地撲著自己褲子後面的右口袋及又一再指著這個人褲子後面的右口袋，明顯地表示出他無意傷害他及他所要的只是他的皮夾而已。

Suddenly, senior Wang thought of the late Chinese-American movie star Bruce Lee who used his Chinese martial arts to deal with the criminals in Kung-fu movies. Since the young man held his wallet, the young man should be a criminal. Because senior Wang had also learnt some martial arts when he was young, maybe simply because he was so much over-confident of his martial arts ability, in the next few seconds, senior Wang swiftly jumped in front of the young man and stopped him with a pretty good Kung-fu posture which he learnt from a Bruce Lee movie. Afterwards, he used his right hand hastily and repeatedly patting his own trouser's right back pocket, then pointing at the young man's back trouser pocket. It indicated clearly that all he wanted from the young man was nothing else but his wallet, without any intention of hurting him.

這個突然的奇怪而又強有力的動作把這個年輕人嚇壞了。他開始說了一些聽起來不像是英文的話語，可能是西班牙語，不管什麼語言，王老完全不懂。雙方沉默了一下，這個人似乎終於明瞭了這個東方老人的意圖，他緩緩地將他的皮夾從褲子口袋中掏出並舉了起來。當王老點頭後，他迅速將皮夾拋向王老，然後以儘快的速度逃之夭夭。

The sudden, strange and powerful action stunned and frightened the young man. He began to speak some kind of language, not sounding like English probably Spanish for which senior Wang did not understand at all. Finally, after a long minute, the man seemed to comprehend what the elderly Oriental man meant. He slowly took the wallet out of his pocket and held it up. When senior Wang nodded, the man threw the wallet at senior Wang and then swiftly ran away.

完全用自己的方法將遺失了的皮夾收回到他褲子後面的口袋裡，這個快樂的中國老人找路走回他兒子和媳婦的家中，一時意氣高昂就如同功夫電影裡的真正李小龍一樣。

With his stolen wallet returned to its home in his right rear trouser pocket by all of his own way, the happy old Chinese man found his way back to return to his son and daughter-in-law's home in a highly triumphant mood as though he were the real Bruce Lee in a Kung-fu movie.

在客廳裡，王老興奮地告訴他的妻子、兒子亨利、媳婦玖蒂他是如何勇敢地從一個黑色頭髮的年輕男子處奪回了他被偷去的皮夾。

In the living room, senior Wang was so excited to tell his wife, his son Henry and his daughter-in-law Judy how he bravely retrieved his stolen wallet from a young man of black hair.

"爸，"玖蒂立刻高聲讚揚，"您的行動簡直就和功夫電影理的李小龍一模一樣。"

"Dad," Judy praised loudly and immediately, "you acted just like Bruce Lee in a Kung-fu movie.."

讚揚使得王老爽朗地笑了

That made senior Wang smiled broadly.

"我們是多麼地爲您驕傲，爸，"亨利擁抱著他的父親大聲笑著說。

"We're so proud of you, Dad," Henry hugged his dad and said with laughter.

王老開心了。他很高興大家的注意力都集中在他的身上了，因爲他完全用自己的力量把他的皮夾弄回到了他的褲子後面口袋中。

Senior Wang beamed, pleased with the attention being lavished on him and satisfied for his forceful action to get his wallet back in his pant's pocket where it belonged.

奇怪的是他的妻子這次竟然沒有像他們結婚四十多年來的習慣而一言不發。她快速走去他們的臥房然後又回到客廳，手上拿著另一個正方形的黑色皮夾。她告訴她目瞪口呆的丈夫，當他出門去散步時，她在地毯上發現了他的皮夾，明顯地因爲他口袋上面的扣子鬆掉了，皮夾滑落在地上而他還不知道。

Strangely, during all this time, his wife did not say a word as the way she had been in their over 40 plus years of marriage. She quickly went back to their bedroom and soon came out with another black leather square wallet in her hands. She told his stunned husband that she found his wallet on the carpet after he had gone out for a walk. Obviously, his pocket button got loosened and the wallet slid down on the ground without his realizing.

　　一種使人不舒服的沉默突然籠罩著這整個客廳。大家都很難過地明瞭了這是怎麼一回事情了，這位一向行爲端莊的臺灣退休政府官員恐嚇搶劫一個無辜的青年，只因爲這個人撞巧也有一個和他的一模一樣的皮夾，搶奪來的皮夾裡面只有幾張美國一元鈔票和兩個墨西哥披索。

An uncomfortable silence suddenly fell over the whole room. They were all dazed as they realized what had happened. The usually mild-mannered, retired government official from Taiwan had frightened and robbed an innocent young man who happened to have a wallet that looked exactly like his. The obtained wallet by force contained only a few one dollar US bills and a couple of Mexican pesos in it!

　　煞那間，這位中國老人的面孔漲紅而他的心跳也加速，他把自己拋在沙發上閉上了眼睛呈現著極度尷尬和羞愧。他不像李小龍，像功夫電影裡被李小龍痛毆過的一個大壞蛋。

Sunddenly, the senior Chinese man's face flushed and his heart beating rapidly, he dropped himself on the sofa and closed his eyes in a great embarrassment and shame. He was not like Bruce Lee now, but a bad guy badly beaten by Bruce Lee in a Kung-fu movie.

煙　蒂

Cigarette Butt

　　每一個認識 Tony 陳的人都同意 Tony 是個精幹的成功商人，他擁有兩家大的"假日旅舍"連鎖旅館，一家在休士頓，另一家在奧克那合馬市。不管當地的經濟如何變動，這兩家旅館的業務仍然非常平穩。因此 Tony 經常來往於這兩個都市中。

　　Every one who knows Tony Chen agrees that Tony is an astute and successful businessman. He owns two large franchised Holiday Inn hotels, one in Houston and the other one in Oklahoma City. And the business of the two hotels keeps prospering despite the local economic situations change. Therefore, Tony goes between the two cities all the time.

　　二十五年前，Tony 從臺灣來美國留學，註冊在休士頓大學主修工商管理，課餘在一家汽車旅館裡打工為櫃檯業務員。於獲得工商管理碩士學位後，他在休士頓市中心區一家"假日旅舍"連鎖汽車旅館裡找到了一個全日工作，櫃檯服務部經理。三年後，他被提升為該旅館的副總經理。旅館的老闆也就是總經理也是從臺灣來的一個老人。Tony 工作非常勤奮，不久，他就獲得了老闆的全盤信任。

Twenty-five years ago, when Tony was a foreign student from Taiwan studying at the University of Houston, he worked part time at a motel as a front desk agent. After earning his master degree majoring in hotel and motel management, he soon found a full time job as the chief front desk agent at a franchised Holiday Inn in downtown Houston. Three years later, he was promoted as assistant general manager. The owner and general manager was an old man also from Taiwan. As Tony worked very industriously, he soon won his boss's full confidence.

七年後，旅館老闆感覺年老力衰不能再繼續經營這麼一個大的企業，乃與 Tony 達成一項協議，將旅館賣給他而不要他的頭款，除了接著按月付給銀行貸款外，並於每月付與賣主一筆款項爲期二十五年。因爲旅館業務一直賺錢，Tony 迅即接受了這筆交易。

Seven years later when the owner felt too weak to manage such a big enterprise, he made a deal with Tony to sell the business to him without down payment. Besides assuming the regular mortgage loan, Tony would have to pay the ex-owner a certain amount of money each month for a period of twenty-five years. Since the hotel business always kept in black on the book, Tony accepted the deal immediately.

Tony 的妻子 Silvia 王來自香港，也是休士頓大學的畢業生。在沒有嫁給 Tony 前，她和他在同一汽車旅館裡工作同事好幾年。

Tony's wife, Silvia Wang, was from Hong Kong, also a graduate of the University of Houston. She had worked with Tony at the same hotel for several years before marrying him.

變成旅館主人後，這對夫婦檔日以繼夜地努力工作，旅館業務蒸蒸日上。五年後，當奧克那合馬市內另一家“假日旅舍”連鎖旅館出售時，這對夫婦向他們的銀行要求貸款成功，又將之買了下來。於是這對夫婦檔變成了兩家大旅館的主人。

After becoming the hotel's owners, the husband and wife team worked almost day and night, and their business surely went on more prosperously every year. Five years later, when another franchised Holiday Inn in Oklahoma City was offered for sale, the couple went to their bank and without too much trouble obtained a loan and bought it. The husband and wife now became owners of two large hotels.

他們仍然住在休士頓，可是兩人每個星期至少去奧克那合馬市一次，與他們派在那裡的總經理檢查各項業務之進行。幾乎每次都是在他們的旅館裡過一夜，第二天早上開車回家。慢慢地，Silvia 厭煩了這種旅行不想去了，讓 Tony 一個人來回。日子久了，她索性連休士頓的旅館也不去了，在家做個全職的家庭主婦。她與她的丈夫生有兩個孩子，都是男孩，大的已經進入大學了，小的仍在中學裡讀書。兩個男孩都住在家中，受到他們母親的親切照顧，使得做父親的可以全心全力投入他的旅館業務。

They still lived in Houston, but he and she traveled to Oklahoma City at least once a week to check the business with their general manager over there. Most of the time, they would spend one night in their hotel and drive home the next day. Gradually, Silvia became tired of such travel and decided to stay at home, letting Tony go alone. As time went by, she even chose not to go to the Houston hotel either. She enjoyed being a full time homemaker. She and her husband had two children; both are boys, one in college and the other one still in senior high school. Both of the boys lived at home under their mom's close watch and care while their dad was busy with his hotel business all the time.

他們聘僱的奧克那合馬市假日旅舍總經理是位女士，名叫 Helen Jones。她原來是那家旅館的櫃檯部經理，任職多年，這對夫婦檔 Tony 與 Silvia 於接手後乃提升她為總經理。Helen 碧眼金髮，像貌秀麗，四十出頭，離婚多年，與前夫沒有生下一男半女，因而得以全力投入她新的職位，由於精明能幹，顧主及部屬之間的關係相處得極為愉快。

The general manager they hired to manage the Holiday Inn in Oklahoma City was a woman, Helen Jones, who had been the chief front desk agent in that hotel for many years before being promoted by the new owners, Tony and Silvia, as their general manager. Helen was an attractive blonde in her early 40s, divorced for several years and she and her former husband had no children, so she poured herself into her new assignment. She was very capable knowing what she was doing and always doing a good job. So the relationship between the owners and their general manager was pleasant.

一天晚間，當 Silvia 準備去參加一個社交派對時，她突然發現她的汽車發動不起來了。因爲她急於忙著離家及 Tony 那天晚間沒有出門的計劃，她乃開著他的車子去赴會。會後她送一位女性朋友回家。這位朋友喜歡吸煙，她問 Silvia 她可否把車窗放下抽根煙。Silvia 說她和她的丈夫從不吸煙，可她還是同意讓她的朋友抽根香煙。

One evening, when Silvia was going to attend a social party, she suddenly found her car could not start. As she was in a hurry and Tony had no plan to go out that evening, she drove his car to attend the party. After the party, she offered a female friend a ride home. The friend was a smoker. She asked Silvia if she could smoke in the car with the window down. Silvia said that both she and her husband never smoked. Yet she still gave her guest consent to smoke one cigarette.

當她的客人把車子上面的煙灰缸拉開後，她告訴她的駕

駛朋友她發現一根煙蒂在缸裡。Silvia 很驚訝，她把煙蒂撿
了起來，發現這是根已經燒掉了一半的 Slim 牌香煙，在煙蒂
一端還留有輕微的口紅印子。明顯地表示這另一個吸煙人也
是位女士，於是她告訴她的朋友，這一定是在她丈夫帶他商
業上的女性吸煙朋友去開會或者像今天晚間一樣送她回家時
她所留下來的。

When the rider pulled out the ashtray in the car, she told
her driver friend that she had found a cigarette butt in it. Silvia
was surprised and indeed picked up a cigarette butt and found
that it was a half-burned cigarette, brand of Slim, stained with a
slight red lipstick print at the end. Obviously, the other smoker
was also a lady, so she told her friend it must have been left by
her husband's female smoker business friend when he was
taking her to a meeting or her home like what they were doing
that evening.

一個煙蒂上面有著紅色的口紅印子發現在他丈夫的汽
車煙灰缸裡！這位女性吸煙人是誰？Silvia 那天晚間回家後
沒有去問她的丈夫，可這個發現一直蕩漾在她的腦海裡，一
直到上床睡覺時還感覺不太舒服。因為除此以外並沒有發生
任何其他端倪，時間久了，她也就把這件事情忘記了。

A cigarette butt with red lipstick print was found in her
husband's car ashtray! Who was the female smoker? Silvia did
not ask her husband that night when she returned home, but the
thought still lingered in her mind which did not make her feel

comfortable when she went to bed. As nothing else happened, she eventually forgot this event.

兩個月後，當 Tony 要他的妻子和他一起去奧克那合馬市主持他們接手假日旅舍兩週年的慶祝派對時，Silvia 欣然同意。

A couple of months later, when Tony asked his wife to go with him to Oklahoma City to be charge of a party in celebration of the second anniversary of their purchase of the Holiday Inn in that city, Silvia was glad to go with him.

在派對裡，她又遇見了他們的能幹女總經理 Helen。Silvia 很快就發現 Helen 是一個吸煙者，而且她所吸香煙的牌子和她在她丈夫的汽車煙灰缸上撿起的煙蒂是同一個牌子。眼看著 Helen 迷人的微笑及她那誘惑的身材以及她和她丈夫談話時的親密態度，有時後更用手輕拍著他的肩膀，突然間她驚駭莫名，幾乎想立刻返回她休士頓的家中。她那往常一直掛在臉上的笑容也不多見了。Tony 很敏感，他很快就發現了他妻子的不愉快神態，他問她怎樣了，半出嫉妒半出憤怒她冷淡地回答沒有什麼，要他不要擔心。Tony 不明瞭他的妻子為什麼突然會不愉快。

At the party, she met their capable female general manager, Helen, again. Silvia soon found out that Helen was a smoker and that the cigarette she smoked was the same brand of cigarette butt she had discovered in her husband's car ashtray.

Seeing Helen's bewitching smile and striking figure and the intimate way in which she talked with Tony and occasionally patting him on his arm, suddenly, she was aghast and almost wanted to leave for their Houston home. And naturally, her usual smile on the face was not as often as the way she used to wear. Tony was sensitive. He quickly noticed his wife's uncomfortable behavior and asked her if she was all right. Being jealous and somewhat angry, she coolly replied she would be all right and asked him not to worry too much about her. Tony couldn't imagine why his wife so suddenly seemed upset.

　　會議完畢後，他們改變原來想在奧克那合馬市旅館住一宿的計劃，當天晚間就開車回家。在回家的途中，Silvia 一反常態，一言不發，這使得 Tony 更爲擔心，他也不好問什麼，只有把心思放在心中而專心去開車。

After the party, they changed their plans and drove back home in the same evening, not to spend one night in their Oklahoma City hotel. On the way of going back to Houston, Silvia was unusually quiet which made Tony worry further, but he kept his concerns to himself and concentrated on his driving.

　　Silvia 雖然閉口不語，可她的心中一直存有一個疑問：*是否可能她的丈夫和他們的離了婚的動人女總經理有過生意以外的關係？至少 Helen 曾經搭過一次他的車子，那是無可*

*置疑的。他曾經把她帶去什麼地方做過什麼不可告人的事情嗎？*由於除了那半根煙蒂外，她並沒有發現任何其他的證據，因此她實在不願意去訊問他什麼，因為多少年來他們的婚姻關係一直是非常地美滿。假如她問了，她害怕她會損害她們平和的婚姻即使是一點點她也不願意。

Though Silvia was not speaking, her suspicious mind continued to ask the question: *could her husband and their attractive divorced woman general manager have had some out of business relationship? At least Helen had sat in his car once that was sure. Did he take her somewhere to do some hard-to-tell-others affairs?*" Besides the half-burned cigarette, she had no other proof of such a relationship, so she could say nothing to him and she hated to ask him as they had always enjoyed their conjugal happiness. If she asked she was afraid it might jeopardize their peaceful marriage, even just a little bit which she did not want to have.

時間就是這麼樣地一天天地過去。逐漸地，她發現每次 Tony 離家去奧克那合馬市時，他總是細心地挑選那最適合的服裝像襯衫領帶等等就好像他在婚前赴她的約會一樣，她的心開始下沉；不過因為沒有他外遇的確實證據，她還是什麼也不能做。

As time went by, gradually, she noticed that every time when Tony was leaving home for the Oklahoma City hotel, he would deliberately select his classiest suit, shirt, and tie like he was going on a date with her before their marriage. Her heart ached, but without solid evidence of his having an affair, she could do nothing.

又是一個月過去，一件意想不到的事情發生了。Tony 告訴她他們的奧克那合馬市旅館總經理 Helen Jones 辭職不幹了，原因是她遇到了她中學時代的親密男友，這個男子最近也離了婚，他向她求婚，婚後帶她去維金利亞州居住，因為他在那裡有個穩定的工作。突然間，Silvia 感覺如釋重負。她甚至於對她曾經懷疑過她丈夫的忠誠有一種罪感。

Another month passed and then an unexpected thing happened. Tony told her one day that their general manager at the Oklahoma City hotel, Helen Jones, resigned because she had met her high school sweetheart who had a divorce lately. He had asked her to marry him and they would move to live in Virginia where he had a nice job. Suddenly, Silvia felt much relieved and relaxed. She also felt guilty for ever doubting her loving husband's faithfulness.

可是六個月後，有一天她又因故開她丈夫的汽車去參加一個晚會，那是她的休士頓香港培德中學校友會在一家五星級飯店舉行一年一度的聚餐年會。在汽車裡，她無法控制她的好奇心又去檢查一下他車中的煙灰缸。很奇怪她又發現了半根燒掉的 Slim 牌煙蒂，及煙頭上印有紅色口紅的印子，和上次發生的一模一樣。煞那間，嫉妒、憤怒、和疑惑一起湧上心頭，比她第一次發現這麼一個煙蒂時更爲強烈。

But six months later, for some unforgotten reason one day Silvia had to use her husband's car again. She went to attend the annual dinner party for her Hong Kong Pei-De High School Alumni in Houston at a five-star restaurant. Once in his car, Silvia couldn't fight her curiosity and took a look in the ashtray. Strangely enough, she once again discovered another half-burned, branded Slim, cigarette butt with a red lipstick print on it. Everything happened just like the first time. Her jealousy, anger and suspicion all returned even more strongly than it had the first time when she had found such a cigarette butt.

莫非他們以前的那位秀麗的女總經理 Helen 仍然藏身在奧克那合馬市？是 Tony 的陰謀詭計故意編造出來一個什麼與中學時代親密男友結婚後搬去東岸的故事來欺騙她的？她非常憤怒感覺到受了莫大的傷害，計劃那天晚間回家後一定要好好地和她的丈夫大吵一架。

Could it be that their former attractive female general manager Helen was still hiding somewhere in Oklahoma City? Was it Tony who sophisticatedly created the stories of a so-called her high school sweetheart wanting to marry her and move to the east coast in order to cheat her? She was furious, hurt and debated finally confronting her husband after she returned home that evening.

在派對中，她意外地遇到了以前中學裡的最親密同班好友 Sheila 周。遇到最親密的同班好友快樂極了，因而把她原來想和她丈夫吵架的計劃暫時放到一邊去了。兩個女子不停地互相訴說自從四分之一世紀前在香港畢業後的種種際遇。Sheila 說她的丈夫於三年前過世後，她很幸運地通過了針灸醫生的考試，現在奧克那合馬市從事這種古老的中國醫療行業。

At the dinner party, she happened to meet, Sheila Chou, her most intimate classmate in high school. The happiness of meeting her most intimate friend made her temporarily forget her plan of fighting with her husband. The two women had a long conversation bringing each other up to date on their lives since they had graduated a quarter of century before in Hong Kong. Sheila told Silvia that her husband had passed away three years earlier. Luckily, she had passed the examination to become a licensed acupuncturist and now practiced the ancient Chinese medical arts in Oklahoma City.

Silvia 告訴 Sheila 她和她的丈夫擁有兩家旅館。一家在休士頓，另一家在奧克那合馬市。她要 Sheila 把她在奧克那合馬市的地址告訴她。

In turn, Silvia told Sheila that she and her husband owned two hotels, one in Houston and the other in Oklahoma City. She asked Sheila's living address in Oklahoma City.

"因爲休士頓的亞裔人口比奧克那合馬市多很多，" Sheila 說，"我已經決定搬去休士頓。那就是爲什麼我今天晚間來這裡。我正在準備在這裡買棟房子。以後我們就可以時常見面了。也許有一天，我可以見見你的丈夫。"

"Because there are many more Asian immigrants in Houston than Oklahoma City," Sheila said, "I've decided to move to Houston. That's the reason why I'm here tonight. I'm looking for a house to buy. So, we'll spend more time together. Maybe one day I can meet your husband."

Silvia 很興奮，她也急著想把她的同班同學介紹給她的丈夫。"他今晚在家。假如你願意，我把你帶回家去見見他。"

Silvia was thrilled and she was also eager to introduce her former classmate to her husband. "He's home tonight. I'll take you home to meet him if you like."

"那可好啊！" Sheila 高興地回答。
"That would be great," Sheila happily replied.

"會議很快就要散了，" Silvia 說道。
"This party should be over soon," Silvia said.

散會後，Silvia 把 Sheila 帶回家來見 Tony。
So, after party, Silvia took Sheila home to see Tony.

　　沒有人會相信當 Silvia 將 Sheila 介紹給 Tony 時，這兩個人同時都大笑了起來，他們說他們早已在奧克那合馬市相識了。

　　Nobody would believe that when Silvia introduced them to each other, both Tony and Sheila laughed at the same time and admitted that they had already met in Oklahoma City.

　　事情是這樣的。當 Tony 無意中看到 Sheila 在報紙上的廣告中說她的針灸不但能幫助病人減輕痛苦而且也能幫助抽煙人戒除抽煙的惡習，於是 Tony 帶著他旅館裡最年老的員工一個有四十年抽煙習慣的 Mary Ford 去到 Sheila 的診所看看 Sheila 能否幫助 Mary 戒除尼古丁的惡習。第一次不是很成功，可是第二次終於使 Mary 再也不想抽煙了。Mary 含淚感激地告訴她的老闆他簡直如同救了她的一條性命。

　　The true story was that when Tony happened to read Sheila's advertisement on the local newspaper that claimed that her acupuncture not only could help a patient release many kinds of pain, but also could help a heavy smoker quit smoking. So Tony took his oldest hotel employee, Mary Ford, who had smoked for more than forty years, to Sheila's clinic to see if Sheila could help Mary kick her nicotine addiction. The first treatment was not very successful, but the second one was, totally eliminating Mary's desire for cigarettes. Mary tearfully thanked her boss saying that he had almost saved her life.

"你曾經讓 Mary 在你的汽車裡抽過煙嗎？" Silvia 問 Tony，語氣有點怪怪的。

"Did you ever let Mary smoke in your car?" Silvia asked Tony, the tone of her voice like ice.

"是的，有過兩次，都是在去看 Sheila 的時候。" Tony 回答道，他在奇怪她的妻子怎麼會問這麼一個問題。

"Yes, she did it twice on the way to see Sheila," Tony replied, wondering what would prompt his wife to ask such a question.

突然間，Silvia 笑容滿面地跳上前去緊緊地抱住 Sheila，她告訴她，"我真為你驕傲，你做了一件了不起的事情！"

With a broad smile on her face, Silvia suddenly jumped up and hugged Sheila tightly. She said to her, "I'm proud of you. You did a great job."

接著 Silvia 又給 Tony 一個擁抱。

Then Silvia gave Tony a hug too.

Tony 和 Sheila 可能永遠也不能解釋 Silvia 的行為，更不會理解為何她突然變得如此興奮，因為 Sheila 不過曾經幫助一個旅館年老員工戒除抽煙的習慣。

Neither Tony nor Sheila could explain Silvia's behavior and neither would ever realize why she had suddenly become so excited, as all Sheila had done was but to help an old hotel employee quit smoking.

全書完

End of the Book